Ethical Leadership in Sport

Ethical Leadership in Sport

What's Your ENDgame?

Pippa Grange

Ethical Leadership in Sport: What's Your ENDgame?

First published in 2014 by
Business Expert Press, LLC
222 East 46th Street, New York, NY 10017
www.businessexpertpress.com

ISBN-13: 978-1-60649-810-1 (paperback)
ISBN-13: 978-1-60649-811-8 (e-book)

Business Expert Press Giving Voice to Values on Business Ethics and Corporate Social Responsibility Collection

Collection ISSN: 2333-8806 (print)
Collection ISSN: 2333-8814 (electronic)

Cover and interior design by Exeter Premedia Services Private Ltd., Chennai, India

First edition: 2014

10 9 8 7 6 5 4 3 2 1

Printed in the United States of America.

With love and thanks to my dear Donicka and Amalia Birch, who gave me a magic green pen to help me write my first book.

Abstract

Ethical Leadership in Sport: What's Your ENDgame? is a practical guide on how to navigate the complexities of ethical leadership in sport, recognizing the increasing pressure placed on individuals and organizations in sport to ruthlessly compete to win, and at the same time to be exemplary social role models. Most leaders know right from wrong, but giving voice to your values isn't always straightforward. This book explores how to approach the ethical decisions, dilemmas, and value-based conflicts that emerge for leaders in sports organizations in order to make good choices, drive a sound culture, and reduce the risk of going awry.

The approach is twofold: Coaching for the leader on how to make and act on an ethical decision when faced with a dilemma; and an exploration of those deep personal values and beliefs about self and sport that inform how the leader thinks and acts. The book considers ethics in the context of modern sport and highlights the classic ethical traps and cultural slippery slopes to avoid using case studies and examples.

Ethical Leadership in Sport: What's Your ENDgame?: An ally in knowing how to become and stay a leader whose integrity can be trusted.

Keywords

ethical leadership, ENDgame, culture, sport, organizations, winning, social responsibility, role models, ethical decisions, dilemmas, value-based conflicts, leadership coaching, values, beliefs, ethical content, ethical traps, integrity

Contents

Introduction

This book is written as a conversation between you, an existing or future leader in sport, and me, an ally who can offer guidance on how to navigate the practical complexities of ethical leadership in sport.

I am fortunate in my consulting practice, to have had many such conversations and the richness of examples and insights in these pages, is owed entirely to those clients and collaborators who have had the courage to struggle to be better.

I have approached the *ethics* part of this discussion from two angles: the technical and the personal. The technical part is about knowing how to make a decision and enact it consistently in a way that helps you feel confident. The personal part is about considering what really matters to you as a person, who you are, what you believe is good and right, and the very essence of your own values.

When I talk about leadership throughout this book, I am talking about something distinct from, but connected to, authority.

Authority in sport is essential. It maintains the everyday status quo, creates order, and manages and protects systems that get things done. Authority lets us know who is in charge, where the buck stops, and where to go when there is a problem. It is roused when we hear a call-to-arms, when we respond to a crisis or escalate an issue, or when we simply need technical know-how and credibility to proceed. This is the same at half-time in a game of football or in the boardroom. We need these controls to prosper in sport and to stay accountable to our various roles on and off the field. We need "go-to" authority figures or "bosses." Authority is about roles; it is possible to see the scope of a person's authority and where it starts and finishes. You can logically say, "no, that's not my job" when something sits outside of your technical remit or is beyond your role. The team doctor, a respected authority figure, would quickly lose authority when it comes to coaching the game and vice versa should the coach start taking medical decisions. There are boundaries to authority.

I see leadership as something much more adaptive, opportunistic, and with fewer boundaries. If authority is about maintaining control and order, then leadership is about change and progress; a vision to leave things in a better state than we found them. Leadership needs to ask the questions "for whom?" and "why?"

I believe that leadership in sport is necessarily about social impact. It should always embody and represent a much "bigger game" than winning on the day—a higher purpose that is in part about sports people being everything they can be, and in part about making a generous contribution to humanity. We ought to have a vision for an ethical future for sport that we are both proud of and inspired by. We should be unafraid to aim high on standards of integrity and excellence and ambitious beyond the scoreboard. To create such a vision, we need ethical leaders who are prepared to look beyond themselves today and accept the responsibility of making a positive difference to society in the various ways they are capable of. It is difficult to defer responsibility for leadership, and certainly for ethical leadership if you embody such a vision. Saying "it's not my job to do better" is impossible for leaders.

We have to question whether we have the focus and commitment needed in this area at present. Sport has been under fire in recent times as a hotbed of poor ethical choices, underwhelming integrity, and in some cases straight out corruption. Common problems have included the normalizing of harmful practices that put people at risk physically or psychologically, various forms of deceit and fraud that amount to cheating, avoidance of social responsibility on tough human rights issues both within the ranks and in the community, and a win-at-all costs mentality that leaves a chosen few bathed in gilded glory but many more as collateral damage along the way.

It has been argued that the very nature of competition, pitting rivals against each other in a battle for supremacy and gain, will necessarily bring out the worst in a flawed and self-interested human nature. Competitive sport results in a victor and loser, but it does not necessarily have to involve the destruction of the latter or a dismissal of values and principles along the way. It is not inevitable that the test of our own mettle, dominance, and skill in the metaphorical "field of battle" will result in moral poverty. In fact, it is this very test that may offer unparalleled opportunity to display who we are at our best.

Our best nor our worst is guaranteed. Leaders have to cultivate, nurture, and model the outcomes they want. As a leader, you have an opportunity to define and illustrate the better side of human nature in your organizational culture and practices as a start point. A focus on ethics can help you do so.

Being ethical means more than simply identifying moral issues that exist in our various life situations. We can only claim to be ethical when we follow the identification of these moral issues with ethical actions and behavior, those that we think are the right, reasonable, and best course of action in the situation. Such ethical actions are based on a framework reflecting our personal beliefs, our understanding of the contexts in which we operate, and the choices that we have. ENDgame is written to support you in that exploration.

The St James Ethics Centre in Sydney, Australia, notes that the central question of ethics is "what ought we to do?" and whenever we are faced with that question, we are dealing with ethics. They also highlight some "enduring truths" about ethics:

- Ethics is about relationships.
- It is about struggling to develop a well-informed conscience.
- It is about being true to ideas about who we are and what we stand for.
- It is about having the courage to explore difficult questions.
- It is about accepting the cost.[1]

My objective is to help you to feel prepared enough to handle value conflicts and ethical dilemmas when they come along in your professional life (and they will). In so many other aspects of organizational leadership we readily consider what competencies we need to prosper and what strategies and knowledge we need to manage inherent risks. It is just the same with ethics. Being a competent ethical leader does not always mean avoiding ethical risks, they are normal and likely; knowing how to anticipate, prepare for, and mitigate ethical risks is a better objective.

So what do those who get it right do?

- They understand what is happening around them and their own "bigger picture" principles and values.
- They understand themselves and their own likely responses to ethical dilemmas.
- They know a "slippery slope" trap when they see one.
- They understand ethical rationalization, distortion, justifications, myths, and other excuses for not acting.
- They think strategically about "how to" act in the face of conflicts and dilemmas, not "whether to" act.
- They "rehearse" the possibilities so that they feel more confident.
- They learn to communicate about values openly and clearly even in the face of countervailing pressures.
- They create choices and then follow through.

It is not always easy to act on your values. It is not even always possible. It can be particularly hard when you feel alone or isolated, conflicted with others with whom you would really rather stay on side, or if everyone else in the room thinks you are making a mountain out of a molehill. It is always easier, in the short term, to "kick with the wind," but frankly, anyone can do that and I presume you are reading this book because you want to do better than that.

There are, however, times when it is possible to act and get a result, and for those times, it is worth trying. A classic sport maxim is that the "one-percenters" count, the small everyday things, as well as the great challenges, all contribute to fantastic performances. It is the same with building your capabilities as an ethical leader within your organization. The grand moments or genuine catastrophes are few and far between, it is your everyday will and skill that count the most.

There is currently a strong narrative around the importance of culture in sport, and while we may hear the term *values* more frequently, it is actually ethics (which encompasses values) that sits at the heart of the culture of an organization. Your culture helps you answer the question "what ought we to do?" and culture is something you can shape to your advantage.

The reason culture is on the agenda is that the connection between it and performance is being more fully recognized in sport. There is a new emphasis placed on the environments in which athletes live and the systems in which they operate as determinants of ethical behavior. It is no longer an adequate lament that sport simply attracts some "bad apples" and spoiled brats who need pulling into line, nor that "boys will be boys" and this is just the way it has been since time immemorial. An ethical, high-performing culture needs to be cultivated and sports leaders at all levels need to be innovative in their thinking. There is a dawning understanding that it will take more than the carrots or sticks to get people to keep performing and to keep striving for excellence. Athletes like everyone else want something to believe in, a vision that they can invest in and an organization that they are proud to belong to.

It is hard to overemphasize the importance of organizational culture on performance. Research across industry shows us that those organizations with excellent high performing cultures, so massively outperform others, that they are a class unto themselves. Even in the early days of research into organizational culture, John Paul Kotter and James L. Heskett showed, in a longitudinal study over 11 years, that profit increased for organizations with excellent cultures (756% increase versus 1% for others) and share prices increased (901% versus 74% for others).[2] Kotter and Heskett, and many since, believe that organizational culture is probably the most important single factor in determining long-term success.

And the good news is that the single biggest influence on a high performing culture is you, the leader. My question to you is: How will you use that opportunity? A good starting point is recognizing that your worst enemy in ethical leadership is you shrugging your shoulders and saying "so what, not my job...."

How the Book Is Organized

My experience has been that the development of deep understanding on anything requires us to be availed of the whole context and that the context shouldn't be "dumbed-down" or skimmed-over, particularly if the topics get sensitive. For this reason, this book offers a broad context by starting at the edges with the introduction of concepts and theories in ethics, and then working in to the sharpest focus—what you can do to improve. We work forward from thinking about what you believe about sport, its meaning and its possibilities for society, to what you think matters in terms of your own values, principles, and ethical beliefs, including what can get in your way of being and doing what you say you want to be and do. We will then explore the "slippery slope" traps to look out for including what you can hear, see, and feel when they are pending and what you can do to lower the risk of falling into those traps and staying there.

There are several layers of understanding to work through en route to becoming a better ethical leader in sport. Working through these layers will take you from here (capable, with plenty of life experience to draw upon, but maybe somewhat uncertain), to there (an effective and trusted ethical leader). The layers are as follows:

- Raising your awareness of the ethical content in sport.
- Understanding the various component parts of ethical thinking and decision making.
- Highlighting traps that you need to avoid.
- Exploring choices and options that you have when you want to act and trying them out for yourself.
- And finally, putting you in the center of the picture as a leader who walks the talk.

Think of *Ethical Leadership in Sport: What's Your ENDgame?* as your guide to working through the layers.

ENDgame is also the name of the central decision-making framework that I will introduce to you in Chapter 2, and refer to, in later case studies. Like most frameworks, it is to be used to assist you to work through a problem practically and clearly. I hope you will refer to ENDgame many times in the face of tricky ethical dilemmas that land on your doorstep as a leader.

I encourage you to approach the topics within these pages with an open mind and consider your own experiences throughout this book, because they, more than anything in these pages, will be your greatest guide once you have some context.

Ethical leadership in sport is much more than knowing right from wrong on the big issues. It is highly likely that in most cases you can work that out already. Instead, this book is about giving you every possible opportunity to perform well as a leader in this space by anticipating problems, communicating expectations, and developing strategies based on considered thinking.

I hope you enjoy the journey.

CHAPTER 1

State of Play

Check-In

In an April 2013 article about the abusive behavior of an American college basketball coach toward his players, Dr. Keith Ablow, a psychiatrist and member of the Fox News Medical A-Team, declared that sport does not matter:

> Sports, including college sports, have displaced far more meaningful activities and passions in American culture and led to the excusing of horrible behavior on the part of its participants....
>
> Here's the truth about sports of all kinds: They are fun, entertaining, money-making activities that showcase the human spirit of competition at an exquisite level and that don't matter to the world, in the long run, when it comes down to it, at all. Not one bit. Not an iota....
>
> It's time the world of sports and sports fans got over themselves. They are a glaring symbol of how little passion of their own people have now, how much they need to be ceaselessly entertained and how willing they are to settle for being fans, instead of fanning the flames of their own passions....
>
> We'd be far better off, in fact, if all sports coverage was relegated to specialty publications and stripped out of daily newspapers and daily news broadcasts. Because games are games are games. They don't matter. Not really. Not at all. Not one bit. Not an iota.[1]

Dr. Ablow's point is that we give sport per se too much credence over pastimes that he believes would serve us better culturally. I disagree, because what can serve us well culturally are those everyday practices and activities that we are collectively engaged in and in which we can find personal meaning. The issue is what we have allowed sport to become.

I declare my hand upfront in saying that I believe that sport matters. And if bird-watching were consumed in the same broad, public way that sport is today, I would think it mattered to the fabric of society, too, and I would probably be encouraging ethical leadership in ornithologists. This chapter explores "why" sport matters, and the meaning of sport in modern life for many of us.

Whether you love it or loathe it, it is hard to deny sports' presence, visibility, and capacity to engage us. Opinions on the relevance of sport certainly swing from the assertion that sport is in fact the substance of life, to the more moderate view that sport is no more than a benign and trivial distraction from our daily struggles. Somewhere in the middle of these polarities, it seems reasonable to suggest that sport is a factor in how we experience life and our identities as individuals, local community members, and national citizens.

The struggles, victories, contests, catharsis, freedom, rules, connection, territorialism, tribalism, heroes, and villains of sport hold up, in some part, the mirror to the day. From this angle, sport seems more "essential" than just a game. It matters because we decide to care about it, and we expend emotion on it—good and bad. That care may be directed toward the uncertain fortunes of your team this weekend and the likelihood of making the play-offs, or to the ethos your child develops through his or her soccer training, or perhaps to the role sport plays in keeping you active and well. On the flip side, maybe your care is demonstrated as moral outrage, disappointment, or abject disgust about the failures and flaws of sports' personalities. It could be that you care about the national investment in something as benign and unimportant as "games" in comparison to education, literacy, or the arts, for example; or perhaps you are incensed at the use of sport as a political lever and vote-winning platform for politicians. Regardless, the presence of it in our lives requires "psychological investment" and as soon as we care about something, it holds meaning.

We probably should care more about global economic collapse, terrorism, climate change, and overpopulation in the world, than about sport, but that doesn't make sport meaningless. Sport can offer "treasured meaning." The point is that it isn't automatically positive or full of truth and beauty, nor is it inevitably vapid, corrupt, and self-serving. Sport doesn't automatically maketh the man any more than it will turn an otherwise cultured young person into a competitive thug out for his or her own glory at anyone else's expense. We each decide what meaning we will give to sport, what care we will invest in it, and how we will use what is essentially an empty container waiting for our input. What sport means depends on what we do with it and how we use or abuse it.

Perhaps then, sport is more a reflection, than a driver of who we are.

Why Does This Matter?

When you remove your blinkers and consider what sport means, and to whom, you might see a much greater responsibility than what happens within your organization, club, or team that accompanies your role as a leader in sport. This can be a little overwhelming. Didn't you sign up to be part of a sport and entertainment business? Isn't this supposed to be "living the dream," your childhood best-case scenario for earning a living while having maximum fun? When did sport get so serious and so scrutinized?

It would be a luxury to think that you are supposed to be just winning football games, gold medals, lucrative stadium deals, and broadcast rights and not be worrying about the shape of your integrity and whether you are seen as over privileged or over paid, whether your attitudes are outdated, racist, homophobic, or sexist (for example), or whether your private choices stand up to public scrutiny. You could get on with the job and not take yourself too seriously. But when you stand back and consider that some people may think that you are partly responsible for nation building and the common good, and should be a role model for young people on moral issues (a role you may have considered to be the domain of parents and school teachers), things get a little more confusing.

Whether you are a current or future leader in sport, you will face ethical dilemmas, value conflicts, and integrity challenges as you pursue your vision, and those value clashes might be with others and within yourself. Examples, small and large, abound.

Should you allow an athlete to continue to compete in your sport when you have it on good authority that he or she is using a banned substance but hasn't been tested and only one or two other people know? Does your decision change depending on the athlete—what if it is the team superstar? Does your decision change depending on how close you are to the finals?

Should you send a national representative athlete home from international competition for conduct that was less than expected from a community role model, but closer to dumb than illegal?

Should you reprimand one of your Olympic national athletes who favorably affected the outcome of fellow national athletes (in another sport) by providing information regarding opposition injury, given by accident in an administrative mix up? What if no-one knows except you and your team?

Should you address a sexist comment made by one of your athletes, off the field, that was recorded on a mobile phone at a bar by a member of the public and sent to the media?

Should you allow one of your superstar athletes to use his or her brand, achieved through the sport, to sell merchandise with slogans that undermine some of the sports' social messaging, for which it receives significant government funding?

Should you accept a fast-food company as a team sponsor who is offering to triple your current sponsorship bottom line when you know it will result in the end of an existing contract (with a year to run) with a health promotion agency because the existing sponsor cannot continue to invest, given the conflict of interest?

These are not straightforward challenges, especially if you are unsure about your organization's (or team's) purpose, values, or principles; they require consideration on a number of levels, and significant responsibility rests on the shoulders of the leader.

The best way to face the very real responsibilities of leading in sport is to see sport for what it is—good, bad, and ugly. Sport is no silver bullet for fixing the problems of society, improving people's quality of life, or for single-handedly developing character in people. Nor is it detached from these possibilities. Sport is quite simply what we make it. The more you understand the context and meaning of sport in modern life, as something greater than the next contest, entertainment, or the trivial pursuit of a few, the better equipped you will be to navigate as a leader, whether you agree that the mantle of social responsibility is unreasonable and idealistic or otherwise. Expect the inevitable value conflicts and you may be able to relish the possibilities for progress that they bring.

In this chapter we will explore two topics that shed light on the context and meaning of modern sport. The first explores how we arrived at this position today, where sport seems to be falling down ethically more than ever, and in more areas. The second is a look at how sport offers meaning in society at various levels, with a specific look at Australia as a case study.

Discussion

Context 1: New Business, Old Ethos

The integrity of sport has been challenged on many levels in recent times with concerns around doping, match fixing, gambling, illicit drug use, and other criminal activities as well as concerns around a lack of care for athletes and their well-being. One proposition about why this is the case suggests that sport has started to lose its identity, and the tension between old and new sports' values is bubbling to the surface.

I see modern sport as a bit like an adolescent; changing, complex, and not entirely sure of who or what it wants to be in the future. It is both a fast-moving lucrative entertainment business with as much commercial exchange, consumer analytics, growth agenda, drive for profit, brand artistry, and political jockeying as any other industry, and at the same time, unlike many other industries, sport is a much loved, oft lamented source of personal and social identity for many people (who don't necessarily work within the industry).

It seems that sport and business are now irrevocably intertwined. It is certainly a successful economic marriage. But could some of the current malaise in the culture of sport be about a mismatch between the deeper philosophies and values of sport and those of a commercial business? Is sport supposed to be about outcomes, exclusivity, gain, and glory or is it supposed to be about process, inclusivity, growth, and sacrifice? Which values hold true in the systems, structures, and symbols we create for sport, and which ones sound good in the rhetoric but are fairly flimsy, if not false, when tested out (like when winning or losing is on the line)?

History offers us some insights into the possibility of mismatched values. Although notions of individual ethos, glory, strength, and valor in fact motivated the ancient Olympics (it was largely about heroes), I find it more useful to start with the Victorian era for the purpose of this discussion. It was at this moment in time that the identities and purpose of both sport and business started to crystallize in the way we understand them today.

Although the concept of sport, or games, is much older, the word *sport* comes from the Old French word *desport* meaning "leisure," with the oldest definition in English from 1300 being "anything humans find amusing or entertaining." It was at the whim of the individual, unconstrained, unimportant, and unashamedly self-pleasuring. It was just for fun, and understood as "just a game." It could be argued that sport was invented *Ad Captandum Vulgus* (to please "the mob") and only the trappings have changed today; we are just more likely to see the mob in matching franchise merchandise and be able to get a hamburger at the coliseum.

Sport may have been at its origin something raw and trivial, but by the mid-19th century, it had become corralled and used as something more purposeful. British history gives a sociological account of sport being used to prepare young men in public schools to go forth and rule new lands. It was seen in part as a way of building the character that would be needed for the exercise of empire. People needed to have winning attitudes if they were going to conquer the world … and where better than the sports' field to gain such training? So sport became systemized around zealously guarded ideals that reflected the times politically, socially, and economically through this Victorian era. It was no longer about individual gain, but about collective strength. Sport was organized, and amateurism was born.

From then, this organized, character-building display of spirit and talent called amateur sport began to represent the twin ideals of strengthening citizenship through participation and enhancing nationalism by fielding successful teams in international competitions. It melded the upper class desire for social hierarchy with the middle-class belief in education, self-discipline, and social responsibility: the amateur ideal has always been to improve individuals *and* society not only by instilling the values of hard work, team sacrifice, and fair play, but also by inspiring community pride with inspirational performances. Thus amateurism in the Victorian era started to associate the sporting contest with a philosophy about how we ought to live, and indeed, who we actually were in a national sense.

So it was around this time in sports' history that the idea of individual sacrifice and the greater good took hold (pretty useful if you want people to have the character to go forth and rule on behalf of the empire without losing sight of Queen and country), and those earlier notions of pleasure, leisure, and personal gain were looked down upon (not so useful for the purpose at hand in the mid-19th century). It was no longer about you, or you alone at least, and certain values became privileged or favored in sport, such as loyalty, teamwork, sacrifice, integrity, stoicism, grace in victory or defeat, and so forth. We even developed a name for those privileged values: sportsmanship.

Sportsmanship is supposed to express an aspiration or ethos that the activity will be enjoyed "for its own sake." The well-known sentiment by sports journalist Grantland Rice that it's "not that you won or lost but how you played the game" and the modern Olympic creed expressed by its founder Pierre de Coubertin "the most important thing ... is not winning but taking part" are typical expressions of this sentiment.[2]

Then things became more complex toward the end of the 20th century as sport began to professionalize. One of the key differences between amateur and professional sport, of course, is that in professional sport, participation is incentivized. Money and personal gain were introduced, and along with them, some additional, or perhaps reordered values. Modern professional sport is big business. Semiprofessional sport in the form of the Olympics is big business, too. Sport appears to be in the midst of a struggle to uphold the noneconomic values (in fact anti-economic values) on which amateurism was founded, and to reconcile the motive for profit and personal gain that underpins the modern business of it. The two motives are poles apart.

It's important to highlight here that business is not the "bad guy," nor are the values that underpin business any less worthy. Potentially, the traditional values of sport and those of commercial business run into conflict, and I suspect that unless the sports industry reflects on these value conflicts in a more considered way, the two philosophies may continue to grate and we can expect to see the industry saying one thing, doing another, and struggling to maintain the appearance of integrity. This won't help in effective ethical decision making.

We have considered conduct within commercial business and enterprise for longer than we have considered conduct within sport. There is a great deal of evidence of both activities in ancient Roman times, and from the start there was consideration about what was fair and right behavior for the individual when trading. Since then, ethical considerations have been debated in management theory and philosophy across the Eastern and Western worlds ad nauseum. William Shakespeare's *The Merchant of Venice,* which is believed to have been written between 1596 and 1598, describes a commercial ethical dilemma!

It's fair to say that the spin put on the enterprise of business has historically been much less favorable than the spin put on sport, however. Historically, the merchant in Shakespeare's play is a good representation of the way that commercial activity—goods and services exchanged for money—had been seen as somewhat unsavory. This may have roots in notions of social hierarchy, where the wealthy were considered to be virtuous, noble folk who did not soil their hands with commerce, and business was seen as a necessary evil in society.

So what does support the ethos of business and how might it clash with the ethos of sport?

One of the foundation principles of modern business is the notion of free will: we are free moral agents, able to make decisions, control our own destiny, and engage in a social contract. This notion has been much celebrated in the idea of the entrepreneur as someone who freely decides to pursue a risky venture in the hope of receiving great rewards.

Another philosophic principle that would become part of business theory and practice is rationality—the idea that we fundamentally do what is best for ourselves. This is partly the basis of capitalism—that we will regularly make choices that are about our own self-interest and we're in it for ourselves at the end of the day (though that does not necessarily have to be at the expense of the other).

On the one hand we have the ethos of sport in amateurism, where noble self-sacrifice, the representation of other citizens through your endeavors, moral conformity, and playing for the love of the game are culturally dominant. On the other hand, we have the ethos of commercial business, where free will, definitions of success based on individual (or organizational) gain, independent enterprise, and playing to win are culturally dominant. Neither sport nor business were built on unethical foundations, but perhaps we have not paid sufficient attention to how their respective purposes come together: where they gel and where they clash. Is sport for the greater good or for individual gain? Can it be both and stay ethical? Does the old ethos still fit with the new enterprise?

Both sport and business grapple today with whether ethical conduct is the responsibility of the individual, the organization, or the industry. There is a big clue to this struggle in the fact that sport continues to try to get people to comply with rules, respond to imposed values, and behave themselves, rather than engage in a deeper and more useful conversation about ethics, namely what matters and why. Corporations in which owners have limited liability face similar challenges. Can the business of sport continue to outsource blame to individuals when faced with ethical failures? I argue that it is time to play a bigger game.

Context 2: Half a Dozen Reasons Sport Matters

What does sport mean to us and to society other than offering a trivial pastime and entertainment? If sport was indeed invented to please the mob, it has achieved much more.

My home, Australia, is a country where sport has certainly achieved economic, social, and cultural prominence. In a recent piece of commercial research that I undertook for a large organization wanting to understand how sport worked as a means of building social capital for new migrants and refugees, I found some very strong opinion on the substance and meaning of sport in Australia.

I have presented six themes here as an Australian case study that are informed by the thoughts of a diverse group of people, from migrants to government ministers, who spoke to me about what they believed sport meant in Australia. Of course, there will be differences across cultures: Case studies on Brazil may reveal greater emphasis on the role of sport in the national identity, in Sweden we might see an emphasis on health, in

South Africa on community connectedness, or in the United States on economic impact and entertainment. Nevertheless, the Australian themes can offer some general insights.

One: Sport Means Positive Economic Impact and Community Benefits

The Frontier Economics Report on the economic contribution of sport to Australia nominates three main ways in which sport delivers benefits to the Australian economy outside of dollar value generated directly through sports services.

First, *community level sport* is considered to be good for our physical health. It promotes physical activity with benefits in terms of reduced health-care costs and improved labor productivity. Research from the report shows that health costs could be reduced, in gross terms, by \$1.49 billion per year and that productivity gains, by making the workforce healthier through increased physical activity, could be as much as 1% of GDP (or \$12 billion) per year.[3] The Australian Bureau of Statistics (4156: 2012) states that almost two thirds (65%) of Australians aged 15 years and over participated in physical activities for recreation, exercise, or sport at some time during the previous 12 months, and of the children aged 5 through 14 years, a massive 60% participated in organized sport outside of school hours during the 12 months ending April 2012.[4]

Second, community level sport accounts for a disproportionate amount of community volunteers, which has been shown to have a positive impact on health, socialization, and social cohesion of the Australian population. Not only that, it is a significant part of producing champions! Volunteer labor is involved in every aspect of the sport pathway with the labor input of volunteers valued at around 4 billion per year.[5] Sport and physical recreation organizations attract the largest number of volunteers with 2.3 million people (37% of the population) in 2010.[6] The ABS (6285: 2010) found that an estimated 1.6 million people (9.9%) aged 15 years and over were involved in nonplaying roles such as coach, instructor, or teacher; referee or umpire; committee member; and scorer, timekeeper, and other support roles.[7] It is arguably part of the glue that connects communities.

Finally, the international success of *elite Australian sportspeople* has had a significantly measurable positive impact on personal and community well-being; a great sporting success is one of the most tangible things that could make us feel good personally and collectively—the value of which is calculated to be in excess of the entire current annual budget for elite sports (roughly $20 per household per year).[8]

In direct economic terms, today's global sports industry is worth between €350 to €450 billion ($480 to $620 billion) per year. This includes infrastructure construction, sporting goods, licensed products, and live sports events.[9] Australian households spent over $8.2 billion on selected sport and recreation products in 2009 to 10.[10] That is certainly a direct economic impact.

Two: Sport Supports a National Identity

Theoretically, sport offers a visual demonstration of national character and strength. Some believe that the Australian identity has been forged in war and sport in equal measure, but as war on a global scale has faded in recent years, perhaps the demonstration offered through sport has become highlighted.

Sport seems to be Australia's national theatre in the way politics or religion is in other places. What goes on *within* Australia is the essential drama of the place as unlike Asia, Europe, or North America, geographic isolation provides the country with a blissful insularity that translates into fervent interest in the goings-on of sport. Even as Benito Mussolini was on the rise as a cult figure and hero in Europe in the 1930s, Australia's national heroes at the time were a cricketer and a horse!

The traits and behaviors that we favor in our sporting heroes are perhaps not so different to the traits we favor in our national identity: those that we believe have helped us survive and flourish. In Australia, this is about sticking together. For early settlers, the character and resilience of the nation rested on what people believed they had in common and that commonality allowed them to prevail. The romanticized image of an Australian was an image of a hardy, stoic, and determined individual who stuck with the task and stuck with his mates, and the values that were part of this Australian identity were carried through to the field of play. Today's Australian sportsmen and women, deemed to have "let the team down", are treated with uneasy disregard, while those who sacrifice themselves for the team are considered favorite sons and daughters, thus perpetuating the rose-colored national identity.

Sport may also be significant in the Australian identity because the opportunity to succeed within sport is perceived to be a product of variables that are about your genetic talent and your character rather than your birth into a socioeconomic group. This "fair-go" opportunity feeds what some have called the *Australian egalitarian myth* where all-comers are seen to enjoy an equal chance to succeed.

At the same time, elitism (specifically body elitism) is wholly accepted within sport in Australia and we are comfortable celebrating those who physically stand out from the rest, thus offering a pathway to admiration (and a means to become integrated in to the national identity) for culturally and ethnically diverse people that may be otherwise more difficult to achieve. Indigenous Aboriginal and Torres Strait Islander people, as the first Australians, continue to struggle to achieve social equality in Australia across education, employment, health, and prosperity, and yet in sport, Aboriginal people have had opportunities to demonstrate their abundant talents on more equal terms. Indigenous Australian playwright Wesley Enoch summed up the "exemption from exclusion" that sporting talent brings when he said, "no one ever asked Cathy Freeman to run slower."[11] Freeman is much loved as a representation of a successful and talented Australian and her Gold Medal win at the 2000 Sydney Olympic Games was seen as a source of national pride and a symbol of progress for Aboriginal people.

However, our national identity, who we see ourselves as, gives rise to some challenging ethical questions and these are not divorced from sport. Culture, sport, and passions can be a powerful, sometimes highly flammable mix. Who is invited and welcomed into sport? Is this visual demonstration of our national character an honest and accurate reflection of who we really are today? Should it be? If sport is in some small way a reflection of national identity, we might also need to ask, "What do we want to see in that reflection?" Sporting glory is almost always about domination in the moment and sport is characterized by hierarchy and by superiority. We value and recreate these things through sport. It has in many instances played a role in reproducing violence, division, and exclusion along racial, ethnic, gender, and other lines. Any role that sport can have in developing or deepening the better part of our humanity, or any reconciliatory role that sport can play therefore, is not seen as automatic, but as something that needs to be cultivated in Australia and elsewhere.

Three: Sport Offers Symbolism

Sport plays an iconic, symbolic role within Australia, which is played out around events (e.g., the Melbourne Cup horse race as a public holiday, the Australian Football League Grand Final event, the Bells Beach surf event, and the Australian Open tennis). These populate the Australian calendar and the news landscape and are structured into our communication as quintessentially important to Australia.

We use sport as a powerful and permeating way to define what we know about the country. We consider sport to be "ours," part of "us." Food could be considered to be too much a part of everyday life, arts too marginalized, politics too conflicted, and business too global to be iconic to Australia. Organized sport is seen to be British, and ultimately Australian, in the same way opera is seen to be Italian. Even those people who are uninterested in or dislike sport will often agree that in Australia, it runs up and down the spine of the country.

Four: Sport Can Connect Families

Sport is home to a range of traditions within families, within communities, and on a national scale. The ABS (4174: 2009–10) reports that 43% of the adult population attended at least one sporting event as a spectator during the last 12 months, and so often sport is a pastime for families.[12] It is one of the cherished activities that can link us: grandparents and their grandchildren, fathers and their daughters, and men and women within families.

A research participant told me a story about watching his son first manage to kick a football correctly after hours of practice. Although it did not change his respect or love for the child, he described feeling an incredible sense of satisfaction that they were now bonded in a social way on something that could be shared for the long haul. He felt that it somehow galvanized them as father and son and gave them a common touchstone. Another participant talked about how she would always go to the football with her dad when they had something difficult to talk about, so they could raise the topic in between screams and moans and cheers and direct the emotion either of them felt to something palpable in the game: they did not even have to look at each other.

Five: Sport Offers a Sociocultural Metaphor

Although sport may be seen as our great distraction, a lot of social issues are discussed through sport and it allows us to explore the social or political topics of the time without being necessarily political or factional about it. It can be subtle and does not need to be legislative on heavy issues, yet it can go right to the heart of the matter. For example, in Australian Rules Football (AFL) the indelible image of player Nicky Winmar in 1993 lifting his shirt in the face of racial vilification to show his black skin as a proud Aboriginal man to be seen and acknowledged, created popular debate about racial discrimination and human rights that contributed to our shifting national values—a debate that is still energetic today.

Sport is part of the discourse of the day in many work places, schoolyards, and social settings and it even achieves an official centrality in the federal government rhetoric in Australia, New Zealand, the United States, and the United Kingdom particularly. It is a useful way to discuss who we are and how we live.

Waleed Aly from the Islamic Council of Victoria has noted:

> The benefit is that sport is largely a meritocracy. Where sport is the vehicle for culture, anyone can jump on board. You do not need a genetic link to the nation's past. Cultural life is not so much about a shared history as it is a shared present.[13]

Sport has an amazing opportunity to allow us to consider and respect differences in culture and yet abide by the laws and rules of citizenship. Australian journalist Martin Flanagan in 2011 recalled a speech he had delivered in the middle of a football ground to a group of young men from multicultural backgrounds, in which he said "this is a footy ground, not a Jewish or Muslim ground. The rules are different out here and if you want to play, you need to play by the rules."[14]

Six: Sport Can Create Community and Belonging

Some would suggest that if you can understand the network value of sport, you can understand how to get on and get into Australia; that understanding sport is important to understanding the Australian mainstream. Sport is an aspect of the dominant culture that is much easier to decode than the rest and thus a starting point from which to explore. It is less complex and in fact less personal than going to a bar for a social drink, for example. There are relatively small numbers of people without sporting connections of some kind in Australia. Australians are well educated in sport. We think about it, we know about it. Sport makes it to the evening news just about every night.

So sport is almost a form of social currency in Australia. John Carroll from Latrobe University in Melbourne notes that the meaningful aspects of connection between citizens are work, education, and sport in Australia, with sport allowing us to express and share passions and values.[15] Sport is self-reinforcing as a critical construct in our culture; it seems kind of *obvious*, with the availability of beaches and parks and ovals everywhere to play sport. It is the color and size of sport in Australia that makes it critical; we are overwhelmingly exposed to it as a representation of what we value culturally.

Author Benedict Anderson described our modern national community as an "imagined community," where a sense of belonging was as important as the physical links to neighbors and neighborhoods that dominated in earlier times.[16] Virtual or imagined communities are enabled by affiliations to sport. In Australia, it is not uncommon to be asked about *your team* before your school or profession. On the surface, it is an obvious place to feel a sense of connection and belonging.

Each of these themes skim the surface on what the substance and meaning of sport is in Australia, and no doubt in many other places. I have barely even mentioned the sheer joy, exhilaration, and happiness that sport can bring to us, but if you need a reminder, just look at the face of any participant: 6-year-old debutante, 50-year-old weekend warrior, Olympic medalist on the podium, or fervent, screaming armchair fan.

Not one of these themes amount to the conclusion that sport is automatically a good thing. We create meaning, and the presence and cultural visibility of sport means that we have many opportunities to create treasured meaning.

Check-Out

This discussion simply provides a starting assertion that to take a position that sport is just a game is unconvincing, and to take a position that sport doesn't matter is implausible. The important questions are—**what's the point of it?, what matters about it?,** and **how can we ensure that we keep it at its best, ethically?**

I believe that we are at a junction in modern sport where we need to reassess what the point and purpose of it actually is. I don't believe there is truly a burning platform and sport is about to sink under the weight of moral ineptitude, but we may have a bit of maturing to do. Reconsidering sport from the position of ethical leadership gives us a good starting place to lead sport to being at its very best, in all its various guises.

- Yes sport is part of the entertainment business, but also part of complex identities and experiences for many people. It intersects with our lives and the communities we live within in myriad ways and even for those who dislike it, it would be difficult to argue that it is irrelevant or unimportant.
- Sport and business face the same challenges around winning-at-all-costs. They may have evolved quite differently but essentially the ethical fork in the road at this point is similar for both, and it is time to broaden the definition of success to include how we "win," not just how often we win.
- What happens in sport may reflect *and* shape what happens in society, with an emphasis on the former. Because it is so readily consumed and so visible, there is an opportunity for sport to lead and shape conversations on culture and ethics that may reach different audiences especially young people in

more "everyday" ways. Other industries or social institutions may struggle to match this reach.

- Sport does not happen in a bubble. However myopic and self-oriented a sport environment may become, the responsibility of sport and especially its leaders has broadened in recent times and excuses that it is just a game just don't wash anymore when it comes to ethical conduct.

Chapter 2 focuses on the various component parts of ethics, and presents our central model, the ENDgame framework, as a guide to ethical decision making.

CHAPTER 2

"Doing" Ethics

Check-In

Sport, typically, considers ethics in two ways. First, through considerations around minimizing problems such as cheating, corruption, scandals, harm, and crime and, second, through considerations around sporting values and aspirations to succeed.

These two approaches go a long way toward thinking and acting ethically, and in many cases, they have transformed sports and sports' teams for the better. Managing problems and risks emphasizes principles as an element of ethics, and aspiration to succeed emphasizes values, but there are other elements to consider alongside, and importantly, they need to be considered together as the overall *ethical content* of situations. Questions such as, what do I believe?, what do I value?, what can I rely on about myself and others?, what conflicts does this bring up for me, or others?, and what commitments, duties, and promises does this call on?, need to be looked at in synchrony.

This chapter *deconstructs* ethics so that the most important elements are clear and accessible for you to work with as a leader, and then *reconstructs* them as the ENDgame framework that you can utilize when you face an ethical dilemma and need to make a decision.

When it comes to ethical leadership, decision making is of course critical, but unless we are happy to stop at an intellectual understanding, we need to move beyond decisions to action. Decisions are just the start of things. Ethical leadership is something that you actually do. Ethics should really be a *doing word*, a verb. A good mentor and colleague of mine, Simon Longstaff, suggested that if a person said "I ethic-ked myself out of a really tricky situation today," it would best represent how to approach the field.[1]

Decision making could be described as the technical or intellectual part of ethical leadership, but the primary skills of an ethical leader are interpersonal. Success as an ethical leader is more often dependent on the ability to experiment with different possibilities, to stay curious about differences in values and beliefs, and to collaborate and partner with others to find a way forward.

Planning how you will act once you have worked out what is the right thing to do is just as important as the decision itself, and so is being confident and equipped to take such action. We talk about both of these later in the book. But first, let's get clear about what "raw material" we should be working with when making ethical decisions.

The deconstruction of ethics is of course somewhat contrived, as the subtleties, knowledge, skill, and intuition involved in the theory and practice of ethics, developed over centuries of human struggle, is extraordinary, and far beyond me as an author or practitioner to fully explain. My emphasis here is on highlighting and helping you to recognize how the various elements that are involved in decision making, such as your own beliefs, biases, values, virtues, principles, and predictions, work together to get you to an outcome.

The ENDgame framework helps you to "do ethics" when you need to work through a dilemma. The framework also considers the critical and often underplayed part of ethical practice that involves staying aware of oneself. This entails not only developing a well-informed conscience about the way you live and your own moral intentions but also recognizing your own biases, inclinations, desires, and fears that contribute to your decisions and actions.

When you first look at it, the framework might seem complex. It isn't, once you consider and get clear in your mind what the E, the N, and the D represent. What are the **E**thical elements I need to think about here? What do I need to **N**otice and recognize about myself in this scenario? And what will I **D**ecide and do, that will work for me in the circumstances? The framework simply guides you through those questions that will be most relevant, without dumbing-down the thinking and without making it so enormous that you need to sit down and have a rest before you start. With some repeat effort, it will be a habit before you know it; these considerations can become the things you automatically draw on as you lead.

I imagine that much of this chapter will be a reorganization of things that you already understand, hopefully in a way that makes them ultimately more usable. There is also some potentially less familiar comment on your conscious and unconscious biases and how they cast light and shadow across what you see.

The conversation is designed to build your awareness of both ethical content and ethical process.

Why Does This Matter?

Sport has been under pressure to become "more ethical" recently, but this hasn't been coupled with the easily consumed, user-friendly information on how to improve your competence as an ethical leader, how to make better ethical decisions, and how to go ahead and act on your values once the decision is made.

The emphasis has been much stronger on investment in the "integrity" of sporting codes and sports organizations. Such investment has been largely focused on improving and enforcing ethical behavior through policy, codes of conduct, frameworks, ombudsmen, integrity officers, and training. Efforts of a more regulatory nature have focused on the creation, communication, and articulation of new rules and standards, against which sports people are monitored and punished for deviance. But rules and training are not enough if we cannot recognize all the ethical content of dilemmas, as they are presented, including our own biases, and if we don't have the confidence to act when we can see an issue on the horizon.

Judging a decision as ethical or otherwise is not usually as straightforward as whether someone has made a clear trade-off between, say, cheating and winning. Take a decision to use a doping substance or method in sport that is not banned by the World Anti Doping Authority. It is technically legal to do so, but not necessarily ethical. If this choice is made only on the basis of whether using the substance or method is within the rules, the questions of what is at stake in regard to the spirit of competition, athlete care, or a range of potential harms are left unaddressed and the issue of fairness is equivocal, only answered in terms of the existing rules. Ethical decisions are best made with as many broad sources of information as possible, and a reliance on your own thinking, not just rules and policies.

The not-banned substance use is the kind of decision that steers you right in to the "ethical grey area," a place where you need to consider the choice carefully in order to avoid grave integrity issues. However, it is not just the large-scale moral quandaries such as this that require attention, it is also the everyday ethical challenges, like giving honest feedback, avoiding situations that can potentially lead to compromise, or continuing a course of action that you know is high risk. A positive ethical climate is created by leaders who focus on the practicalities of ethics, who demonstrate how ethics is part of everyday sporting life, not just something to discuss when a major event or incident happens, or during annual induction training or "integrity workshops."

Many sports organizations have not yet adopted ethical decision-making training, nor do they focus on the ethical content of issues as a normal, integrated part of doing daily business. Ethics has tended to be something associated only with problems, scandals in the public domain, and large-scale issues such as cheating or corruption. It has also tended to be used retrospectively once a problem has occurred. Shifting this focus will not only improve the health of sport generally, it can put you ahead of the performance curve as an ethical leader in your sport.

Discussion: What It Means to Be Ethical

So what is "ethical" anyway? Let's start with some descriptions.

Normative ethics, our focus in this book, is part of the Greek philosophic tradition. You may well recognize some of the early big-hitters in this tradition in Plato, Socrates, and Aristotle, and there are of course many others.

Unlike other forms of philosophy that ask about the nature of truth or beauty or existence, for example, questions that are theoretical in nature, the core question that ethics seems to answer is a different kind of question—a practical one, and that is "what ought one to do?"

The reason it is practical is twofold. First, the question is not about what one ought to feel, think, or be, but what one ought to *do*. Ethics is also practical in a second sense in that if you have concluded that you ought to do something, then you should actually do it, with minimal hesitation. For example, if a fire is burning in a house across the street, and you come rushing out and realize that a couple of children are caught inside the burning house, it is hardly time to convene a symposium for three days to discuss the situation; if you conclude that you ought to rescue the children, it would be remiss to go back inside and say "well that was a pretty interesting chat, let's have a beer." The decision on what you ought to do is just the precursor to doing it. Similarly, if a sports team says that it values respect, its members should speak up or act to stop bullying or hazing of young players. This requirement to act singles out the question of ethics from other forms of philosophy that you can actually talk about for centuries!

The use of the word "one" (or we) in ethics is also deliberate. Ethics doesn't ask "what ought I do?" or "what ought they do?" It asks "what ought anybody in similar circumstances, with similar capabilities, do?" If two people confront the house fire and one is able-bodied but the other has a broken leg or is in a wheelchair, then clearly there is a relevant difference and that should be taken into account. But where there are no relevant differences, if we think in terms of me or him, and not us, we may be at risk of creating self-serving exceptions from the rule that are not warranted. It's easy to stand apart and lament what he, she, or they ought to do, from a psychologically safe place that doesn't require the will or fortitude to act. I explore this a little further later.

The third thing about the question of: What one ought to do? Is that it is imperial in its sway; it applies to everything. It isn't just reserved for enormous topics such as stem cell research or capital punishment, it is just as relevant in, say, the purchase decisions you make in a supermarket, or how you prepare for and play a game of football, or how you relate to your teammates—it really makes a claim to any part of the world in which you exercise your capacity to make a choice. As such, ethics recognizes that much of the world in which we live is a product of our choices. Our lifestyles, the institutions we create, the goods and services we produce, and our behavior as sportsmen and women are all part of the architecture of choice.

So what does it take to be ethical? What do we need to consider? If we followed these big-hitting Greek philosophers Socrates, Aristotle, and Plato, through "a doorway of ethics" to a place, where sport maintains its integrity and becomes all it can be, we've worked out that the beam above the doorway would be inscribed with the question "what ought we to do?" but what would be on the posts that hold the beam up?

What could be so important that it could be relied upon to hold up this central question of what we ought to do? The Greeks looked to geometry for ideas, which begins with something that is true and self-evident: something that is clear, certain, and doesn't need further proof. They asked if there was anything like that in the human condition when it comes to ethics: any single truth that does not need to be proven, and that we can see the evidence of again and again. And they concluded that there was one thing. And that one thing, which is self-evidently true and does not require any further proof, is that when human beings are given an unconstrained choice (no gun at their head or arm behind their back), they will always choose the thing which they believe to be better than other choices. If you give people a choice between a malteser and a minty, those people who pick up the malteser do so because they think it is better than the minty at that moment. They have made some kind of judgment or evaluation of the options and then made a choice. Similarly if you ask someone if they would prefer to fly first class for free on an uncrowded flight, or pay for a full-price economy ticket for a middle-row seat, what are they going to choose? They will choose the thing that they believe is better, right?

So the Greeks say "OK, so this is where we start."

Values

Having worked out that we humans will choose what we think is good or better, the next thing they (and we) have to answer is "what is it we actually consider to be good?" The ingenious Greeks carve the word *values* on the first metaphorical doorpost.

When someone talks about their values, what they are saying to you is that "these are the things I say are good, so you get to check whether or not what I say and what I do are in line with each other". If I tell you that "I value trust," then you are entitled to believe that when I come to exercise choice on something that effects trust, I will choose the option that lines up with what I think is good. But if you watch me behave in a way that is, say, conniving or cheating, or cunning, then you will be entitled to either discount my sincerity about valuing trust or to think that there must be something very flawed in my worldview.

The list of values, that human beings think are good, is broadly similar across human societies. In the absolute list, you will find many terms that are common. In her note "ways of thinking about our values in the workplace," Mary Gentile notes that much research has been done over time and across cultures, and although differences do surface, there is a great deal of commonality among a list of values that most individuals identify as central … and that this shared list is rather short. The values of honesty, respect, responsibility, fairness, and compassion are seen to be common to all of us and almost universally supported.[2]

Similarly, in *Moral Courage: Taking Action When Your Values Are Put to the Test,* Rushworth Kidder describes the extensive areas of consensus on core values he finds in his cross-cultural surveys, as well as in other research, pointing to psychologist Martin Seligman's work:

> There is astonishing convergence across the millennia and across cultures about virtue and strength...Confucius, Aristotle, Aquinas, the Bushido Samurai Code, the Bhagavad Gita, and other venerable traditions disagree on the details, but all of these codes include six core virtues.

The virtues Seligman refers to are: wisdom, courage, humanity, justice, temperance, and transcendence.[3]

However, there are some differences and the differences are in two forms.

One difference is about how a value is expressed in different cultures. For example friendliness and openness in one culture might be symbolized by giving a gift, a ritualized token of esteem such as hard-to-get tickets to a blockbuster game or even money, and in another culture, a gesture of friendliness may be expressed as a willingness to share a meal or a drink together. If two people from these respective cultures are trying to forge a business relationship, and the first person gives a gift, without any cultural context on his values, the second person might think "oh, that's an improper inducement; they are trying to buy favor." It's a sad fact that very few people take the time to ask what the value that underlies that conduct is. This is an easy way to make mistakes in judging ethical conduct. Both people seek the same value of friendliness, but don't realize that, because they don't recognize the expression of the value.

The second, and more profound difference that arises over core values, occurs when values are forced to be ordered in terms of their priority. The ideal would be that all values play their role in harmony, but it's not the case.

Let's look at a cross-cultural example here. If we had a list of values that included things like liberty and harmony and success, and we had done a survey of Americans on 10 September, 2001 (before Al Qaeda mounted its attack), where we asked, " what do you think the most important and the least important value on this list is?" The survey participants may have struggled around some things of course, but it's fair to assume that there would have been an overwhelming consensus in America that liberty was number one. Indeed, liberty is part of the national identity expressed in many ways; the land of the free, the fight against oppression, the right to religious freedom—there are a whole lot of institutional memories and institutional structures (including the constitution and its amendments) that give priority to liberty in the United States.

If we had done the same survey in China on the same day and they had produced their list, we might have found that liberty was in the list, but that it didn't have the same priority as it did in the American list. In fact, we would probably find that it was lower in the list than harmony or order. The Chinese might have said, "Well this business of burning the flag ... we value liberty but not if it is going to throw our society into chaos and confusion! That's not our way of going about things." The differences between cultures and relative value priorities can make a huge difference in worldviews.

These differences in value priorities are not only on a national scale but you can also see them between the athletic department and the management of a sports club, the coaches or umpires and referees and the governing body, the reception desk, and the CEO's office.

So back to the contention that we will choose what we believe is good at any point in time. By 12 September 2001, the day after Al Qaeda did attack the United States, the value of liberty was arguably replaced at the top of the list by the value of security for many Americans (validating the prediction that what we want we will prioritize and choose). The American people were then faced with the choice about whether liberty or security had primacy in their values list. This kind of value shift can alter decisions on many things including laws, infrastructure, military requirements, and political choice. Choices can be dramatically different with a shift in the priority of our values.

In the same way, albeit on a much less grave scale, sports clubs and teams may reorient their values under pressure. They make different choices about what is good and act accordingly.

Consider some classic sports values and how they become conflicted under pressure:

- Mateship versus self-preservation
- Loyalty versus honesty
- Elitism versus inclusion
- Pride versus humility
- Ambition versus self-sacrifice
- Ruthlessness versus respectfulness
- Teamwork versus self-reliance
- Winning versus taking part
- Equality versus insider-group
- Patriotism versus multiculturalism
- Warrior versus role model

Principles

There needed to be a second "doorpost" so to speak, to hold up the question: what ought one to do? The Greeks continued to think this through and concluded that it is not enough to know what is good, because there will be times where, in pursuit of something good, you may do something wrong. You also have to work out what is right.

In sport, success might be very tangible, like a premiership win at the end of the season or a gold medal, and if you ask most people what do you think about your team winning a premiership or a gold medal, they will say, "that is a good thing." But if you ask how they feel about the athletes taking performance-enhancing drugs in order to secure this win, many people may say, "hey I'd like to win the premiership/medal, but that's not right." So, the other doorpost is created by the third question: "what is right and wrong?" and the word *principles* can be carved on it.

Principles basically regulate the means by which you secure what you want or what is good. Pamela Shockley-Zalabak describes the difference between values and principles nicely when saying, "our values motivate us, whilst our morals and principles constrain us."[4]

We recognize principles in things like the Golden Rule: "do unto others as you would have done unto you," or in the sunlight test: "only do those things which you would be proud to see displayed on the front page of the newspaper." The sunlight test is pretty useful because it highlights the difference between how you feel about your actions if you don't get caught and how you feel if your actions are widely known, begging the question "what are you proud to own as your own choice?"

Although closely related (as posts to the same doorway), values and principles are distinct, and yet they need to be used together. The value gives the principle context, and alone, the value doesn't tell you enough to make a decision; "do unto others as you would have done unto you" doesn't tell you what to do! Nor does the sunlight test tell you what it is that you can be proud of. It is the combination of these two things together that gives you the architecture of choice.

The ethical errors that many people make are invited when we only focus on what is good, not what is also right. The focus on good alone can deteriorate into an *unthinking*, end-justifies-the-means position; we win (or get a result), but at too great a cost. The analogy of the policeman who engages in "noble cause" corruption offers a useful description here: "I knew for a fact that they were guilty, but I just couldn't get enough evidence, so the fact I planted a bit of evidence on them shouldn't matter. If I hadn't, they would have gotten away with the crime!" (I often ask my clients to watch the Ben Affleck movie *Gone Baby Gone* as we start to explore ethics because it highlights this scenario—and a range of other ethical dilemmas—brilliantly.)

It would be lovely to think that these things always sit in neat arrangements, but they don't. Values can come in to conflict with each other and principles may not always be perfectly aligned. They are of course varied and not all principles you adopt are apparently noble things like the Golden Rule. You might replace "do unto others as you would have done unto you" with "do unto others *before* they do unto you" and adopt a principle around preemption, which you might think provides you with an ethical basis when you relate it back to your values.

Either way, you need to consider both values and principles in ethical decision making.

Defining Purpose

The *doorway* metaphor is not complete without the actual door, and this is represented by the final question; "what is the purpose that this entity or person exists to do?"

A defining (or primary) purpose is often overlooked in favor of a mission—the goal or task at hand—and yet the defining purpose is critical to understand, when making ethical choices and deciding on what is good and right.

For example, a law firm that didn't include justice or even courage anywhere in its working principles, could be said to be ethically misguided and we would be entitled to ask whether the firm quite "got" the reason for the existence of law firms. It doesn't mean that the law firm will only be ethical if the outcomes it achieves are always right and just, but if justice were not part of what the firm sought to do, its existence doesn't add up ethically.

Similarly, a military formation could be said to not quite "get" the profession of arms and its purpose if they didn't have peace as part of their purpose, albeit secured sometimes by means of warfare (obviously, proportionality principles may come in to play here, whereby forces are bound not to use greater force than that which is necessary to achieve their objective).

So what is the defining purpose of sport? Of your sport? Why does it exist in the first place? Is it to entertain your fans? Is it to strengthen your community? Does it exist as a vehicle to allow athletes to compete and win? Or is it to provide a source of identity and connection for people? As outlined in chapter 1, perhaps the reflection it will take to identify and clarify this in a contemporary sense, as well as a dogged insistence on including values *and* principles in ethical thinking, is key to improving the ethical standing of the sports industry.

Morals

This brings us to the question about the difference between ethics and morality. The thing that is most distinctive about morality is that a moral code, if it is complete, will always have values and principles within it. It includes those things that we have been *taught* throughout life are good and right, either through the way we have been brought up or what has been explicitly described by others. You may actually reach a point where you have adopted your moral code so wholeheartedly that you are acculturated in to it, it never changes or wavers, and you live that way quite simply as a matter of habit, without the need for too much thought at all. You might be kind to people, truthful in your dealings, a loyal teammate who never snitches on a friend, and a whole host of other things just in the same way that some people get up and clean their teeth in the morning.

It's easy to argue that having a society full of people who live such a life of habituated morality is better than having people who live an immoral life of destruction, fraud, or violence, for example. But certainly our main man Socrates would say that morality may be good, but it is not as good as living an ethical life. The thing that marks an ethical life as opposed to a moral life is that an ethical life requires examination. You actually have to think about what *you* believe is good and right and apply it to the circumstances in front of you.

You may be familiar with Socrates' famous statement: "the unexamined life is not worth living." What Socrates is getting at is that human beings, unlike other beings (pretty much every being without an opposable thumb really), have the ability to transcend instincts and drives and to make conscious choices (ethical choices). Socrates believed that if you refuse to examine your life as a human being, perhaps because it is too difficult or too controversial, or you just can't be bothered, it is like living in a house with many rooms, of which possibly the most interesting remains forever locked even though you have the key. He believed that if there is a part of your life that you haven't reflected upon or engaged with, then you have lived a less rich life than you could have, a less than full version of the human experience.

Ethical action is not absolute. It can be affected by our ideologies, beliefs, culture, circumstances, and by our own neurology and human nature. But while it is imperfect in approach and result, the non-negotiable component of ethical action is reflection. Your *reflection* as an ethical person is critical. Ethical behavior doesn't happen by accident, even though positive results may.

It is a continuous task rather than a single journey to understanding. A great way to think of this is to consider that the enemy in ethics is "unthinking customs and habits," the things we do because they are just the things that we've always done. Ethics is active, engaged, and deliberate and it requires thinking; Ethical practice involves a lot of practice.

So morals and morality are extremely valuable grounding when it comes to living a good life, but ethics offers the next step.

Sometimes, we encounter people who veer into "moralism" rather than morality. Moralism is the practice of making judgments about another person's morality. This is of course completely acceptable if you are charged with that responsibility as a lawmaker or judge, for example. In those cases, moral judgment is based on reason and necessity, not *just* on emotion. However, moralism is often recruited in service of people getting what they want or winning an argument, and it is often based on emotional reactions. This misuse of "high ground" is false, fake, or hypocritical; and self-promotional "morality" seems generally designed to put down, intimidate, or terrorize others rather than to be helpful to others. Look out for fake moralists; they are enough to put you off your lunch!

Ethics as a Process

As noted in the burning house example, ethics doesn't need to stay with thinking alone. It is more useful to think of it as a process; one that involves building awareness of ethical content such as, values, principles, your beliefs about your defining purpose, and an understanding of your own morals, and also a process that involves reflection, self-management, judgment, and then the most important part, action. If you can develop competence at each of these things, not just the awareness part, you will have the best chance of becoming a leader who uses ethics well.

I was offered some very useful advice on "doing ethics" several years ago during a session at Duntroon military college in Australia, as part of an ethical leadership program. The advice was that when you have an ethical dilemma in front of you, the first thing you ought to try to do is walk a mile in the other person's shoes. This gives you the best chance of understanding how you would wish to be treated in the same situation, information upon which you should then act. In addition, it was said that one should be as fully informed, as imaginative, as consistent, and as empathetic as possible whenever you face a dilemma.

For me one of the most critical companions to the process of ethics is intention. If you act as you intend to act and follow through on what you say matters to you, there will be far less loose ends.

The process of ethical decision making leads to a conclusion, and that conclusion will usually have a cost (even if your choice is not to act on something). Accepting the cost is part of being an ethical leader. It is often difficult to do so. It often requires moral courage, enough to face disappointing someone, standing tall or standing alone on unpopular issues or decisions, and creating a habit of not accepting the easiest route.

Seeing All the Content

Staying aware of ethical content is also about how you see the decision or problem in front of you. David Messick and Ann Tenbrunsel's work on "ethical fading" offers great insight in this area.[5] The authors ask how often do people readily seek and acknowledge what the ethical content in decisions is, or what the ethical implications of decisions might be. Their proposition is that we often allow relevant information to simply fade into the background as we hone in on other aspects of the situation that are more accessible or more familiar. Business challenges may be more often categorized as legal, technical, or managerial, for example, rather than (in part) ethical and then delegated accordingly, perhaps away from the leader. The classification of a decision affects how it is handled and what comes next in terms of action. What we consciously focus on dictates what we notice. How often do we ask what the ethical content is in the daily challenges we encounter?

Staying Self-Aware

Reflecting on your own "leanings" is central to ethical thinking. This includes your strengths and vulnerabilities as well as your conscious and unconscious biases.

Consider your own values and principles, those things that matter most to you and that inspire you, or alternatively get under your skin in a way that makes you feel the urge to act. When did they become important to you? Where did you learn them—are they yours or someone else's? Have they evolved over time? Have they been tested out (can you rely on them being the most influential behavioral driver when you are under pressure)? Do they match up with how other people describe you and your behavior? How much of what you can list as your values and principles actually represent how you live today?

If you don't consider who you are and how you act, your behavioral choices are likely to be more susceptible to your own unconscious emotional biases. It is reasonable to think that most people in society, including in sport, start the day thinking that they will "do the right thing," make the right choices and on the whole navigate the ethical territory they encounter pretty well. And very often this is the case. But evidence across sport (and life beyond) suggests that we also overestimate our ability to do what's right. We fail ethically in big and small ways despite our best intentions.

James Rest describes the traditional ethical process as moving from moral awareness (what could I do?), to moral judgment (what should I do?), then to moral intention (what will I do?) and finally moral action (doing).[6] However, this traditional approach has been criticized by behavioral ethicists Max Bazerman and Ann Tenbrunsel in their book *Blind Spots*.[7] They suggest that there is a big omission in such a process because it only considers reason and not emotion.

Bazerman and Tenbrunsel argue that "what we know we should do" and "what we actually want to do" can be pretty different and particularly, when under pressure, many more of us do what we want to rather than what we should. They argue, however, that the human mind sometimes leads us to behave in ways that are *inconsistent with our own ethical standards*—our desires (including things we want to avoid, or are afraid of) get in the way of our reason; thus, any sound process of ethical consideration needs to have not only a big dose of self-knowledge but also self-management, as part of it.

There are myriad ways we can go awry ethically if we don't stay aware. This isn't just in sport, although sport offers some fine examples.

Take the familiar case of the media leak in sport.

Frustrated and feeling ignored and unheard over time, an employee observes bullying behavior in the organization that he finds unsavory or even immoral. He feels that the behavior typifies the person who enacted it and there is never any recourse because this person is a bit of an untouchable in the organization—perhaps, quite senior, perhaps very popular. The employee decides to leak the story to the media anonymously, knowing that it will be big news and cause grief for the untouchable. The organization has been under fire recently over a recruiting scandal and the media are zealous in their reporting of the leaked story. The employee feels slightly anxious but also justified because the untouchable has infringed standards of behavior so often that he deserves a penalty. In the employee's eyes the untouchable has to be taught a lesson.

The consequence is bigger than the employee may have expected. Whilst the untouchable is publicly humiliated, the organization loses the high-performing corporate manager because she is tired of trying to sell a brand that is publicly under fire. It also loses a sponsor worth millions over a three-year deal that threatens the organizations financial stability. The CEO is under renewed pressure from the board. He is deeply disappointed and feels that his trust has been breached and calls for an internal investigation that will take weeks, into both the allegations against the untouchable and the leak. Athletes report that they are being bombarded with requests for media comment and interviews and the twitter-sphere is alight with negative comments about the organization and the sport. Finally, the untouchable sits at home on the edge of his six-year-old daughter's bed and tries to explain why she is being teased at school about her dad being a bad person.

It is clear that the employee's behavior in leaking the story to the media was unethical using our descriptions above. He may have acted on emotion, but his actions were considered: he reasoned that it was good and right for him to punish the untouchable.

Much of the reasoning about the rightness of the employee's actions dimmed in the shadow of his own perceived moral high ground. The bullying may have been so inconsistent with his own beliefs about what is acceptable, and so unpalatable, that he felt the need to act on his values. Yet he did not take on the awareness that *he was also harming another person.* This is what Max Bazerman refers to as "bounded ethicality" in *Blind Spots*: the systemic ways in which people engage in unethical behavior without their awareness, even when such behavior appears to be inconsistent with their stated beliefs.[8]

It is unlikely that the employee thought very deeply about the ripple effects of consequence on his colleagues and the sport at large. Sometimes of course there are negative consequences when someone stands up for their values and takes action, and they are part of the cost of doing the right thing. However, the employee's intention may never have been for such a harmful fallout and he may have been genuinely shocked to see himself considered morally questionable by others. He was the guy trying to right the wrong!

The example highlights the importance of stopping to examine one's own intentions, as well as the potential consequences of actions we might take. This is where we need to think creatively about ways to act on our values with the least amount of collateral damage.

Understanding your own "blind spots" is pivotal to making good ethical decisions. One client recently described this to me as recognizing his "Robin Hood" tendencies: that he would buck authority to protect the less fortunate. A noble sentiment perhaps, but shooting people with metaphorical bows and arrows from behind trees, was not making him any more of a credible or trusted ethical leader, nor was it recognizing his own ethical infringements.

In chapter 7 on the role of the ethical leader we explore self and self-view further.

Ethics As a Series of Relationships

There is a point in considering how we live that one has to conclude that being ethical needs to be understood in the context of our relationships with other people, with ourselves, and with our environments.

So much of the joy and pain, thrill and tedium, pride and shame that we feel is in relation to others. As social beings, we spend a large part of our existence orienting ourselves around partners, families, and communities—imagined and real. Our institutions of justice, law and civil obedience, education, medicine, politics, commerce, religion, and of course sport—all hinge on the relationships between people.

If we talk about investing in a good society, it is about relationships. If we talk about building a great organization or team that lives its values, it is about relationships. If we talk about sport being all it can be, we are talking about relationships and even if we just talk about being a better person, it is still about relationships.

Ethics and Sound Culture

What constitutes a sound culture? At its most fundamental, this is a culture that allows, facilitates, and encourages the flourishing of the people within it so that they can achieve their purpose. It is also a culture that is free from oppression, persecution, abuse, or bullying of any kind.

A sound culture is people-focused. Indeed there is no such thing as a *culture* without the people who make it. When an organization has ethics at its core, then it is more likely to express its culture clearly in word and deed. It will be more obvious to people within and without "who you are" and "on what you stand." I argue that this understanding allows you to have the freedom, discipline, and commitment that you need to perform at your absolute peak, today and tomorrow.

I personally believe that a fundamental starting point for a sound ethical culture in any organization is that others should never be used as a means to an end. Even for believers who claim the ends justifies the means in sport (which we look at in the next chapter), the line in the sand for a sound ethical culture for me is drawn on seeing others as part of the collateral damage on the way to winning. A child-athlete should not be used to satisfy a parent's need for sporting glory or status when the child is harmed, unhappy, or compromised in some way. An athlete should not be forced to compromise his or her own integrity and lie in the face of a serious off-field scandal in order to protect the sports' clubs reputation. An injured athlete should not be "required to play" by the coach after a medical assessment rules that he or she is not fit and likely to cause further damage if they do play. A basketball player should not be assaulted and abused by a coach as a way of forcing them to perform for fear of reprisal.

The following example was reported across the United States including in *The Washington Post*:

The recent National Collegiate Athletic Association (NCAA) basketball case where Rutgers Coach Mike Rice was fired after the release of a 30-minute videotape on ESPN that documented the physical abuse and profane verbal assaults that Rice hurled at his own players during practice over a two-year span is a good illustration. Debate raged over the incident. College administrators were said to demand that Rice win, yet pleaded ignorant of his methods. The athletes had very limited rights as nonemployees, their only option being to sit out a year and transfer somewhere else if the abuse did not stop or was not dealt with if raised – in effect translating to a penalization on eligibility. In this case, it has been suggested that no single person in authority acted on the abuse in a way that would stop it.

Liz Clarke at *The Washington Post* reported:

> ...On college campuses that compete in big time sports, football and men's basketball coaches, who bring the bulk of revenue for their athletic departments, often run their teams as fiefdoms. They wield profound power over student-athletes, able not only to revoke playing time but also to revoke scholarships, which are awarded on an annual basis. Their assistant coaches typically serve on one-year contracts and, as such, likely will not dissent if something is awry. As long as the team is winning, athletic directors and university presidents tend not to delve too deeply in to their methods.[9]

The Rutgers case seems to be a clear example of others being used as a means to an end. The well-being of the athlete was sacrificed in order to get results. But to be focused on the well-being and flourishing of your people does not mean you have to take your eye off the prize. You do not necessarily have to compromise success, you have to have the will to ask "is there another way?" and sometimes, this involves re-defining success to be something more than today's win.

Using a Framework to Make Ethical Decisions

Over several years of consulting in sports I have used a model to work through ethical dilemmas with clients, presented here as the ENDgame framework (Figure 2.1). It is based in no small part on what I learnt during the Vincent Fairfax Fellowship in ethical leadership, offered at the time through St James Ethics Centre in Sydney and now through Melbourne Business School in Australia.[10]

It may help you to use the ENDgame framework to guide you through the process of making ethical decisions in your professional (and personal) life. Like all frameworks, it is a "container" for information that helps one to consider all the necessary ethical elements in situations that you encounter. There may be more you want to add and there may be a higher emphasis for you in some areas than others. That is fine—use it as a guide. Clients whom I have worked with over time still refer to the framework as a "check" when they face tricky situations, and even when they are well habituated into doing ethics well, as leaders.

Check-Out

Creating the time and mental space for reflection (which includes the willingness to learn more about one's own fundamental nature, biases, sense of purpose, and moral essence) most certainly contributes to the performance of an ethical leader in sport or indeed any field. Thinking about who you are being and what you are doing can ultimately sharpen your focus and create useful habits. This reflection needs to go hand-in-hand with an understanding of what you are dealing with in terms of the ethical content of situations. Put the two together and you are well on your way to getting a handle on ethics.

There is a small amount of bad news at this point. You know the old saying "ignorance is bliss." Well, once you accept the responsibility of being an ethical leader, you also have to accept the cost. This includes forgoing both the naivety that allowed you to justify, distort, rationalize, and even moralize previously, and alas, the comfort of certainty on many occasions. You are no longer a citizen of the "unthinking mainland" where the old customs and habits of sport are understood and unquestioned, and neither are you an inhabitant (although an occasional visitor) of the fabulous

- What is the context of the story?
- What is the dilemma?
- What is at stake and for whom?
- What potential outcomes/ consequences are there?
- What are the important relationship here?
- What principles are in operation?
- Is there anything that suggests the principles should not be applied here?
- Which of your values are in place here?
- Are there any values in opposition (such as honesty versus loyalty or short term versus long term)?
- Where is duty owed here?
- Can you recognize any "slippery slope" traps?

NEED TO NOTICE

- Are you making any assumptions?
- Have you done anything to test these assumptions?
- Who's responsibility is it to respond to/lead on this issue?
- What information is relevant and what should be ignored?
- How do you personally feel about the situation and the people involved?
- What do you think you would see/feel/ experience if you were 'in their shoes'?
- Are there any hot issues/ likely blind spots for you?

- What would your ideal outcome be?
- What is your minimal acceptable outcome? Acceptable to whom?
- What options have you got, A & B?
- Do the ends justify the means in option A? Option B?
- How do options A & B measure up in terms of your stated organizational purpose, vision, and values?
- What will you choose?
- What approach to voicing this decision will give you the most confidence and get an effective result?
- Do you need to "rehearse" with a sounding board or ally?
- In this decision and process is public knowledge tomorrow, does it sit well with you?

Figure 2.1 ENDgame framework

"island of enlightenment," where people are clear and at peace with all of their choices in life all of the time. Instead you are a traveler, a journeyman or woman, on the "isthmus of doubt," on uneasy but rewarding terrain, and importantly, carving a path for those who choose to follow.

- Normative ethics is a process not just a theory. It is a practical and useful tool to use in good leadership, one that requires regular reflection and investment and can be developed in every person. Aristotle noted that virtues are not something we are born with; we have to work at developing them; the same can be said for ethical leadership as a practice.
- It is impossible to imagine a sound ethical culture where people are used as a means to an end in a way that puts them at risk. Not only does this infringe a person's basic human rights, it is morally inept and dangerous. This happens in small, everyday ways as well as in the more obvious cases of abuse and disregard.
- To judge something as ethical or unethical, we need to reflect on our intention. Ethics is an imperfect art and often involves being in the "messy grey area" where we struggle to find the best outcome. A well-informed conscience, clear intention, and understanding of the ethical content in situations gives us some "ethical GPS."
- We often behave in ways we did not intend to if we don't stay aware, not only of ethical content but of ourselves and our biases and desires. We all get it wrong sometimes. Reflection and learning are critical elements of good ethical practice.
- In the face of ethical dilemmas, you can use the ENDgame framework to ensure you cover all relevant content. This is a "virtual coach" for decision making, but no replacement for real conversation with trusted and experienced sources when you get stuck, and as stated, the decision is just the precursor for action.

You have the process; now let us connect it to what the hundreds of years of philosophy tells us about the theory.

CHAPTER 3

Applying the Big Ideas

Check-In

As part of developing your awareness of the ethical content of issues that arise and knowing which beliefs, and biases underpin your action, it is worth getting a bare bones run down on the five main approaches to normative ethics that you will see most commonly.

The reason it is useful to know this is that ethical theories are the foundation of ethical analysis and the viewpoints that help us make decisions. Once you can recognize where a person is coming from—what theory and principles they are utilizing, you can start to see what matters to them and what they believe is right, fair, and just (including their beliefs about their role in a professional sense). Being able to recognize and also respect where someone is coming from provides an excellent platform for more challenging conversations about ethical dilemmas. It can encourage leaders to share risks and responsibilities across differences and it can highlight common ground and mutual purpose as much as division. Understanding where someone else is coming from also enables us to "suspend" what it is that we may be personally wedded to and remain thoughtful while we lead.

These theories are basically "families of thought" in ethics. Each one articulates a particular perspective (such as predicting an outcome and likely consequences, or following one's duties to others) in order to reach an ethically correct decision. Each also has key terminologies associated with it, some of which may be very familiar to you.

The five theories I want to consider here are:

- **Egoism:** the self and its needs
- **Deontology:** duty
- **Utilitarianism:** overall pleasure or pain for all concerned

- **Ethics of Care:** relationships, vulnerability, and empathy
- **Virtue Ethics:** character

Within each "family" there are some important variations to note. The variations on duty (to whom or what do you owe duty), for example, can lead to very different beliefs. There are also a number of other ethical theories that are not explored here and do not fit in to these families. These include social contract theories, rights and justice theories, natural law theories, religion-based ethics, as well as relativism and universalism.

Although this overview is far from an anthology of ethics, it does illustrate and describe the most frequently discussed theories in business and sport that can support your understanding. It is not intended to do justice to the complexity of each theory, which in itself is a well-developed system.

I am going to use stories and examples wherever possible throughout this chapter to demonstrate how the theories look in practice. Sometimes examples in life present as a choice between "head decisions and heart decisions." Ethical theory along with understanding what matters to you helps you to find the balance between the two.

Consider the following example as a starter:

You are the CEO of a well-known sports organization. You become aware that a senior member of your executive team has been pulled over by the police and charged with driving under the influence of alcohol. She had been entertaining clients at a corporate function and had three glasses of wine after a very long working day. She had not been planning to attend the function, but another colleague had become unwell and you asked her to step in and cover for him. Having gone from her regular day to the function in a hurry, she had not had a chance to eat dinner. This executive is probably your top all-round performer and enjoys an impeccable reputation for professionalism and teamwork. You value her highly as a colleague and friend. She had never had any prior convictions nor had she infringed any company policy. The organization, as ambassador, receives funding from a government road safety campaign and there are strict protocols in place around cancellation and rights to withdraw in the face of public infringements on alcohol and road safety. Your workplace policy on driving under the influence of alcohol is very strict and some states consider driving under the influence of alcohol a serious breach of conduct for which an employee can be terminated.

You value the executive's investment and hard work and want to be lenient or even protective of her, but you also value the road safety sponsorship and respect the company policy and understand that you have responsibilities to act accordingly as CEO.

What would you do? Why would you do it? What does your conscience tell you to do and how does that fit with your obligations? Does the formal obligation to the sponsor override the personal obligation to the executive, if indeed you see one? Or perhaps you think that the consequence to the organization of acting one way is better than another? Or that the pain involved in a decision to terminate the executive is pain just for one person, but the loss of the sponsorship affects many more and thus you are swayed to dismiss her?

Understanding and applying the big ideas from ethical theory to your decision making not only helps you work things out in a consistent and considered way, it helps you explain to other people why you have chosen to act in a certain way—pretty important when you are dealing with sensitive situations like the example here.

Why Does This Matter?

Ethical dilemmas arise when you have to choose between two things you believe are right and good, or where you need to make a choice between two things you don't prefer at all (because there is no better option available). It's not really much of a dilemma if you have a straight up choice between good and bad, or right and wrong (even though it may still be difficult or stressful to handle, the choice part is easier).

The classic ethical dilemmas involve choosing between truth and loyalty, between individuals and community, between short- and long-term outcomes, or between justice and mercy. There are of course many more, but you get the idea—sometimes it is just not enough to value the truth if in doing so you will be disloyal to someone you care deeply about, or to value loyalty if it requires you to lie and place someone or something at great risk.

Knowing the philosophical theories and principles that you and others hold most dear is a great advantage in being able to resolve dilemmas. They will assist you to ask different questions as follows:

- Where do I owe duty?
- What is at stake?
- Who will this affect?
- What consequences can I predict?
- What am I prepared to risk and why?

Theory, in all disciplines, connects you back to what you believe most firmly. It offers something that you can trust because you have thought it through, especially when you are acting under pressure. It is just the same with ethics.

There are two important things to file in your mind about using the theories:

1. **You do not need to "pick and stick" with one theory exclusively**. Even though you are likely to sway toward one theory or school of thought (I most often find I tend toward considering consequences first), you can reference more than one point of view as a way of deepening your considerations—in fact, it is a sound way to develop your own view. If you think "OK, what will happen if I do that?," it is completely sound to then say, "Who will it affect? What have I promised? How does this demonstrate what I say I am about as a person?" and so forth. So if we had a room full of people whom we asked "what ought we to do?" in relation to an ethical dilemma, in every person there is likely to be some kind of mixture of responses, with some being more dominant than others.
2. However, **you cannot "shop" for an ethical theory that suits your needs on the day.** Although few people act exclusively within the doctrine of one theory in all circumstances (probably because it

would be restrictive and impractical to do so), the idea is not that you can scan the options and "retro-fit" one that lets you argue your own position or gives you a foot hold to explain your decision as an ethical one. If you describe duty as fundamental in your thinking because it is convenient to do so, and yet you actually didn't consider duty in your choice, you are not being ethical. Consistency is important.

Sport, like other industries, can move pretty fast. It can also be an environment where issues around ethics are immediately dragged out into full public view through the media, which potentially put leaders under pressure to know the right answer, and make the right choice, right away. This is when we are at the greatest risk of closing down hard topics, acting expediently rather than ethically, and reacting to the immediacy of the situation. Having tried and tested both your thinking and your methods for action gives you a big advantage in this situation.

Discussion: Five Big Ideas

Let's have a look at the five *big ideas* from the philosophy of normative ethics and how they can be applied.

Anecdotally, we might say that the most common, dominant response of around half of the people in a room full of dilemma busters, when asked, "what ought we to do?" would be: "well, what's going to happen? What's the outcome?" That class of theory is called consequentialism, where really the likely outcome of an action will decide the matter. Ethical egoism and utilitarianism both fall into this class.

Egoism

Egoism is the theory that fits most closely with the principles of capitalism that we described in Chapter 1, and particularly Adam Smith's "invisible hand" theory that basically states that if everyone focuses on doing what is right for themselves in an ethical way, we will flourish. Egoism states that **what makes something good or bad, right or wrong,** is that it satisfies your desires or meets your needs. The **underpinning principle** is the concern for the self-interest of the person doing, considering, or being affected by the action, and the **best choice** is the choice that serves *you* best. This isn't necessarily as straightforward as being selfish. It is about a fundamental belief that if everyone looks after his or her own interests, and does the right thing by himself or herself first and foremost, society will be best served. This is what is referred to in the capitalist economy and associated business models as "rational self-interest" rather than a straight-out hedonism.

Egoism claims that we have no moral duty to assist others and it only makes sense to do so when we stand to gain from it. Egoists see no rationale or gain in focusing the slim attentions of humankind on what other people are doing. It is the origin of statements like "charity begins at home," or "look after your own backyard," meaning that you should look out for yourself and those closest first.

Egoism is also focused on the outcome of an action, not the process undertaken to achieve it; the decision as to whether something was ethical will depend on the result.

Egoist's motto: "Every man for himself"
Sport's egoist motto: "In it to win it"

Utilitarianism

One of the best-known theories in consequentialism is utilitarianism, which is largely associated with Bentham, James, and Stuart-Mill. Its simple premise is that human beings like pleasure and hate pain; according to these guys, **what makes something good or bad, right or wrong** is that it produces the greatest amount of pleasure (or the least amount of pain) for the greatest number of people.

The **underpinning principle** is a radically egalitarian one, in that it does not count any person's pleasure or pain as being worth more than another's. You may be a King or a beggar in the street (a major sporting superstar or a rookie), but when it comes to the utilitarian's calculations, neither kings or superstars nor beggars or rookies weigh any differently in the balance. Utilitarians think that in principle, if you could map all of the pleasures and pains, or in Peter Singer's more modern form, all of the preferences and aversions, you could add up the points of pleasure, subtract the points of pain, and make a choice on balance.[1]

The **best choice** to make therefore in the utilitarian's view is the choice that is most useful (has the most utility) in creating the greatest happiness overall. This position requires people to find a means to tally or calculate both the likelihood of a good result and the measure of happiness for stakeholders. Sometimes of course, this is intuitive.

Different versions of utilitarianism focus on either quality or quantity in evaluating happiness. Ursula Le Guin's haunting tale *The ones who walk away from Omelas* is a brilliant description of the difference:

> In the story, Omelas is a utopian city of happiness and pleasure, whose inhabitants are intelligent and cultured. Everything about Omelas is pleasing, except for the city's one atrocity; the good fortune of Omelas requires that a single unfortunate child be kept in perpetual darkness, filth and misery and that all the citizens of Omelas should be told of this upon coming of age.
>
> After being exposed to the truth, most of the people of Omelas are initially horrified and disgusted, but are ultimately able to come to terms with the fact and resolve to live their lives in such a manner as to make the child's suffering worth it. However, a few of the citizens, young and old, silently walk away from the city and no one knows where they go. Whether it is better or worse than Omelas remains untold, but those who walk away seem to know where they are going. In Le Guin's tale the ones who stay consider happiness in terms of the consequence for the greatest number, the ones who walk away perhaps consider the consequence in terms of relative happiness and pain for the child versus everyone else, or intensity of suffering of the child versus the luxury of a happy life for everyone else, or perhaps they come from a different ethical position altogether.[2]

Utilitarian's motto: "The end justifies the means"
Sport utilitarian's motto: "Whatever it takes"

Virtue Ethics

The next group of people in the room are going to say, "well actually we are not so interested in consequences really. When you ask us what ought we to do, we want to know what will become of us if we do this? What kind of people will we become?"

This group of thinkers believes that character is a kind of like a lump of clay that can be molded by every action taken in the world. Progressively, the clay of the character is shaped by our regular actions; and what we do, we become. We are shaped a little more in the form of a liar when we tell lies, and if we tell enough lies eventually we become a liar in character.

This feeds in to Aristotle's notion of virtue, and the role that virtue plays in seeing things as they really are in life. He had three central ideas around virtue. Aristotle believed that a virtuous person has practical wisdom (or "phronesis"). Which means that they "can see things as they really are." A virtuous person is not blinded by their own desires or fears, or by thinking that they are more capable or less vulnerable than they really are; they see things as they are and act accordingly.

Aristotle's second idea was that we can work out what a virtue is because virtues are those things that sit on the "golden mean." Take courage for example. Aristotle suggested that courage sat in the middle of a continuum—the golden mean—between recklessness and cowardice. There is no virtue in recklessly running into the face of danger, and there is no virtue in hiding behind your mates. Courage is seeing the situation for what it is, accurately, and being willing to act nevertheless.

So the virtue theory states that **what makes something good or bad, right or wrong** is that the action itself embodies character traits that are culturally highly regarded, such as courage might be. The demonstration of a virtue is seen as morally good and the regular demonstration of virtues are seen to be character building.

Aristotle's third idea and the **underpinning principle** is that we become a virtuous person by doing virtuous things! You can't just think about being virtuous, you have to get on and act. Pretty straight-forward really!

Virtue ethics also proposes that demonstrating good character traits in turn leads to the greater or lesser realization of the full human potential (what Aristotle described as *flourishing*—to grow, prosper, and thrive). The **best choice,** therefore, is the choice that aligns with the virtuous person whom you strive to be.

Virtue theory motto: "Character is destiny"
Sports virtue theory motto: "It's not the winning it's the taking part"

Deontology

The fourth group of dilemma busters won't be satisfied by being told what the consequences are likely to be, or that virtue is at stake: when you ask them what they ought to do, they want to know, "well what's our duty? Where do our commitments lie?" Just as a utilitarian might think that pleasure, pain, or preferences (as consequences) are the defining considerations of a decision, these people think that the defining consideration is reason, or rationality. These guys believe that what makes us human and distinct, is just our capacity to exercise reason, and **what makes something good or bad, right or wrong**, is that it lines up with what you think your obligations and duties are.

The high priest of this approach is Emmanuel Kant. The idea of reasoning doesn't always have to be deeply philosophical; it can be as straight-forward as asking, "well, what have we promised?" What contracts have we signed and what obligations do we have? Some duties may be a product of voluntary commitments rather than laws, but if that is where the promise is for a Kantian, that is where the duty lies.

These guys are quite indifferent to consequences and character in comparison to duties. Kant's general notion was that when a person asks, "What ought I to do?" They are bound to act according to what he calls a "categorical imperative." This is **the underpinning principle.** The categorical part means that there are no exceptions; it applies in all circumstances, irrespective of the consequences, and it is imperative in that it is a command that must be obeyed, but in this case, a command that we give to ourselves.

In formulating the categorical imperative, the method Kant used was the creation of a *maxim*—a rule that would apply equally to all people in all circumstances. As with the utilitarians, Kant had a radically egalitarian part to his worldview, which is that all human beings are intrinsically valuable, and human beings should never be used simply as a tool, or a means to somebody else's end. Kant's logical form simply makes it possible for maxims to be boiled down to things like: "Are the decisions noncontradictory? Are they logical and able to be universalized?"

William David Ross' version of deontological ethics states that the most important way to work out our *prima facie* duties and obligations is common sense, not just reason (beyond logic to *something more intuitive*). For example, Ross believed that the duty of noninjury has priority over all other duties, such as fidelity, self-improvement, gratitude, justice, making amends or beneficence. This isn't something he believed needed calculating or working out, it was something seen as common sense.[3]

So deontologists, either through common sense reasoning or logical reasoning, put their duties as the highest priority when making choices about how to live. The **best choice** for a deontologist is simply the one that lines up best with your duties.

Deontologist's motto: "In service to humanity"
Sport Deontologist's motto: "Take one for the team"

Ethics of Care

The ethics of care theory, also sometimes referred to as feminist ethics, is based on the notion that to exist we are dependent on others; we are interdependent. It is focused not only on individuals but also on the community in which they exist, proposing that we are reliant on and related to the people and institutions around us (for friendship, provision of services, work, health, etc). At the core of this approach to ethics is the idea that we have a duty of care, a moral obligation, to those with whom we have a special relationship, because this care and protection in turn will underpin a thriving community. Defining *special relationship* is somewhat subjective, but for example it is reasonable to suggest that the junior athlete in the hands of the coach or the employee engaged with the organization is in the kind of special relationship intended by the description.

The ethics of care theory states that **what makes something good or bad, right or wrong** therefore, is that it supports positive relationships and the well-being of other people with whom we have a special relationship. So our final group of decision makers is most likely to respond to the question of "what ought we to do?" by saying, "we ought to do the thing that protects and nurtures people and relationships."

The **underpinning principle** is that what matters most is behaving in ways which *show care* toward those people we are supposed to look after and look out for, and particularly those who are vulnerable, who need support, or who are in a position of diminished power. Proponents of this family of thought therefore say that the **best choice** is the one that supports or nurtures other people, for in turn this is what will maintain a strong community.

These guys might ask questions like: What will happen to person X if we did that? Which option best considers the person who doesn't have much voice or much influence? How will that affect person Y's ability to get ahead, and so forth.

Ethics of Care motto: "I am my brothers' / sisters' keeper"
Sport ethics of care motto: "There is no 'I' in team"

Equipped with these basic categorizations, let's explore one of the most well-known cases of ethical failure in sport over the last ten years: The Lance Armstrong example, to put the five big ideas into context:

In June 2012, the United States Anti-Doping Agency (USADA) announced it would bring charges against Lance Armstrong for systematic doping over a period of many years in the late 1990s to mid 2000s. In August of that same year Lance Armstrong said he would not challenge the USADA findings and he was promptly banned for life and stripped of his seven consecutive Tour de France victories. In late October, the International Cycling Union (UCI) ratified USADA's decision to ban Lance for life and strip him of his seven tour victories.

Questions, however, have been asked as to the role and ethical conduct of cycling officials, particularly the UCI in this period of systematic doping.

The news excerpt sets the scene.

Mired in Armstrong doping scandal, UCI claims "moral' authority" to lead cycling

The Associated Press
23rd of October 2012
CTV News
http://www.ctvnews.ca/sports/mired-in-armstrong-doping-scandal-uci-claims-moral-authority-to-lead-cycling-1.1006812

GENEVA – Mired in a crisis caused by the Lance Armstrong doping affair, the sport of cycling faces an uphill trek to regain credibility.

Still, cycling's top official said the sport can succeed despite the doubts of many, including anti-doping leaders who on Tuesday called for Armstrong-era officials to be removed.

"By the decisions we have taken, it has given us the moral authority," UCI President Pat McQuaid told The Associated Press after the UCI accepted the sanctions that stripped Armstrong of his seven Tour de France titles and all other race results since August 1998.

Skeptics still insist that the UCI protected Armstrong from scrutiny for many years, and was reluctantly forced to disown him by a devastating report published this month by the U.S. Anti-Doping Agency. Across 1,000 pages of evidence, it detailed how Armstrong's teams used and trafficked banned drugs – coercing some teammates into the conspiracy – to dominate the Tour from 1999–2005.

"We really had no option but to make the decision we made," McQuaid said.

McQuaid's denunciation that Armstrong "deserves to be forgotten in cycling" was surprisingly strong after the UCI had previously backed Armstrong's failed legal fight to deny USADA jurisdiction in the case.

"We haven't tried to find a way to defend an icon in our sport – we've accepted reality," the UCI president told the AP. "We've accepted the facts and the facts are there. I'm a pragmatic person and I believe no matter how bad the situation might be, you take the decision you have to take and move forward from there.

"The sport has to take what it can from this and use it as a means to convince athletes that there's no future in doping," McQuaid said.

On Friday, the future of cycling will be shaped at a meeting of the governing body's management committee. On the agenda: how to revise race results, including the 2000 Olympic time trial in which Armstrong won bronze; possible efforts to recoup Armstrong's prize money; handling riders' doping confessions; and restructuring the sport to guard against doping conspiracies.

"Why did this happen?" asked McQuaid, who became UCI president two months after Armstrong's seventh Tour victory. "What is it about our sport that forces athletes to do what they are doing? If we can make changes in the structure which weakens the possibility of athletes and teams getting into doping programs, we will bring those forward."

McQuaid suggested that some ideas he plans to share on Friday will not be popular, with speculation that nine-rider teams at the Tour could be reduced in size.

"They may be unpalatable for the teams and the riders, but we will bring them forward," he said.

What is unpalatable to the World Anti-Doping Agency is that McQuaid's predecessor, Hein Verbruggen, can attend the board meeting as honorary president.

Verbruggen led world cycling from 1991 to 2005 and has been sharply criticized for presiding over an era of rampant doping. Though the USADA report expressed concern at some UCI conduct, it stopped short of repeating unproven allegations relating to Armstrong's urine sample with suspicious levels of EPO at the 2001 Tour of Switzerland and his donations to the UCI totaling $125,000.

On Tuesday, the head of WADA – which has long had fractious relations with cycling – said the UCI had to "take the blinkers off" and examine its past behavior by removing those officials who were in charge during the Armstrong era.

"I don't think there's any credibility if they don't do that," WADA President John Fahey said.

McQuaid defended his UCI mentor at a news conference Monday.

"There is nothing in the USADA report which implicated Mr. Verbruggen in any wrongdoing," said McQuaid, who stated he would not resign and likely will stand for a third four-year presidential term next September.

After five hours of defending his organization, McQuaid directed his most pointed frustration at former Armstrong teammates Floyd Landis and Tyler Hamilton, cheating in the U.S. Postal Service team and cycling's entrenched doping culture.

"They are not heroes," said McQuaid, explaining that he was angered by riders who repeatedly denied doping during their careers and who tried to make money from their confessions.

The outburst conflicted with his earlier statement that "the UCI is listening" and welcomed riders telling what they knew about doping.

"Pat McQuaid's comments expose the hypocrisy of his leadership," Hamilton said in a statement to the BBC. "Instead of seizing an opportunity to instill hope for the next generation of cyclists, he continues to point fingers, shift blame and attack those who speak out, tactics that are no longer effective. Pat McQuaid has no place in cycling."

A mooted "Truth and Reconciliation" commission that could offer limited amnesty to riders and officials confessing to doping is also slated for Friday's meeting.

Asked by the AP who represented a brighter future for cycling, McQuaid pointed to riders such as Vincenzo Nibali of Italy, Geraint Thomas of Britain and Tejay van Garderen of the United States, winner of the best young rider classification at the 2012 Tour.

> "They are looking at what is happening and saying 'I never want to be involved in anything like this. I never want to be near anything like this,' " McQuaid said. "They are the riders who will bring our sport forward."[4]

Think about how this case could be framed using the five ethical theories we have explored. What do you believe is the UCI's ethical responsibility to further investigate the depth of doping in cycling and to investigate the ethicality of the previous administration? Put yourself in UCI's shoes and consider what course of action you might take if you were under pressure to do the right thing as a sport, and if you examine your decision as to whether to deepen investigations from the five vantage points.

What Would an Egoist do?

As a theory, Egoism is focused on the outcomes of our actions and behaviors, rather than the way we achieve those outcomes. If, as an administrator, you believe that the best possible thing that can happen, in the interest of cycling, is that the doping issue is closed down and forgotten, so that the sport can move forward, you may choose to focus strongly on the single perpetrator as the cause of the problem: Armstrong as a bad apple. The egoist believes that people are responsible for their own decisions in the end and if a culture of doping did develop, it is attributable to the choices of individuals, not to the sport as a whole. Similarly, if Armstrong decided to donate funds to UCI, from wealth procured throughout his successful career, then that was a choice for Armstrong and seemingly in the interests of UCI to accept at the time. An egoist may rationalize that it is not in their self-interest (which can extend to include beliefs about the interests of cycling) to take the blame; it will serve no good purpose. The ethical egoist's position might be that Armstrong profited greatly from the sport, he had a fair commercial exchange with it, and is owed no moral duty. It was Armstrong *the individual* (and other dopers) who has been found to be cheating, and he (or they) should take the fall.

The egoist may also want to ensure a sport is profitable, successful, and enthralling, thus returning the greatest reward to individuals and *by extension*, the sport. What is the gain in allowing it to unravel further, then? The recent chapter of cycling that so strongly featured Armstrong has been a big part in "selling" and popularizing the sport to the public, sponsors, and media; the performances of the U.S. Postal team have in fact served the interests of cycling well. Why bring it all undone for everyone because one guy (or a comparatively small group of people) cheated?

An egoist might think that if Armstrong was cheating, that is his problem really and there is nothing to gain in denigrating the sport as a whole. The egoist may also believe that the people in charge currently are in the best position to administer the sport and allow it to be successful, thus further disruption to the reputations, security, or salary of UCI personnel through a drawn out investigation is unhelpful.

It is possible to see that the egoist is valuing rational self-interest and nothing in this position is saying that Armstrong's choice or cheating per se was acceptable—in fact it clearly positions it as wrong in the eyes of the sport. But the issue is attributed to the individual and there is no moral responsibility assumed on behalf of the sport, because they state that the "sport" didn't cheat, nor is there necessarily a position that presumes that the virtue or character of the sport is defined by this case. Only the cheat should be judged from this position.

The ethical egoist would probably not investigate further.

What Would a Deontologist do?

A deontologist would want to think first about UCI's duties as a governing body: who were they to and what did they entail? These duties could include duties toward the cyclists caught up in the fray, to other cyclists, to the general public, to sponsors and commercial partners, to the United States Anti-Doping Authority (USADA) to whose rules they were bound, to the UCI itself, and even to the idea of sportsmanship. Maybe, in working through this analysis, the UCI was able to dismiss some obligations to Lance Armstrong on the basis that his actions in doping meant that the contract between the two had been corrupted. "Working through" may also highlight where some duties are in conflict: in this case, a duty to maintain the success of sport internationally and a duty to be publicly accountable.

As a deontologist you might think about whether you would make the same choices if the athlete in question was someone other than Lance Armstrong, an icon of the sport. Could your choice be universalized? Could you say that you would act the same way if the cyclist were little known? Would you make the same choices if the scandal were not so public but had been brought to your attention in more private circumstances?

Central to the idea of being dutiful would be the reflection on whether any person was being used as a means to an end. Is it fair that Armstrong takes the fall for what has been regularly touted as a systemic cultural norm? Do you have a duty to uncover all cheats in the system? What if you did not do so, are you violating any prima facie duties? Performance-enhancing drug use could lead to long-term medical issues for athletes, how will you consider your duty to protect them from injury or harm?

It is possible to see that the deontologist is valuing his or her wide-ranging commitments, duties, and obligations, regardless of what that means for the UCI officials, the previous administration, or the cyclists involved. They would likely prioritize their duty over other considerations.

The deontologist would probably investigate further.

What Would a Utilitarian do?

A utilitarian would think first about everyone who could possibly be affected by the UCI's course of action and the sort of consequences for them—positive or negative, pleasure or pain. If one person's career, reputation, and potentially their psychological well being is destroyed, even if evidence *were* equivocal, is that an acceptable cost to maintain cycling at the pinnacle of elite competition for athletes and fans of the sport and investigate no further? What if it were the whole of U.S. Postal Team? And what if it were 100 cyclists? How will you weigh the cost of their happiness? What of the sponsors, partners, and fans? What of the UCI employees? How do you rate the well-being of a future cyclist entering the system and culture for which you are the administrator? A utilitarian approach would require a cost-benefit analysis on the breadth and depth of consequences for all involved—you, fellow administrators, cyclists, team officials, sponsors, fans, and so forth.

You could say that a choice not to investigate the potential wide-ranging use of performance-enhancing drugs could be acceptable from a utilitarian point of view because you feel it will have the greatest positive ramification for your sport and the people within it and this would result in the greatest amount of happiness versus unhappiness for those involved.

Fairness as a value and greatest good as a principle are quantified or qualified this way for the utilitarian.

The utilitarian would probably not investigate further.

What Would an Ethics of Care Position Be?

From an ethics of care perspective, the first consideration would be what relationships are at stake in this scenario? This includes both relationships between UCI and the various stakeholders including cycling fans, but also the relationships between Lance Armstrong or other implicated cyclists and their own stakeholders. An example of implications considered from an ethics of care perspective might be the cost to the not-for-profit Livestrong Foundation, founded by Lance Armstrong in 1997, to provide support for people living with cancer. Livestrong recently lost clothing brand Nike as a sponsor in the wake of the scandal.

The ethics of care perspective would also consider the vulnerabilities of cyclists who were enmeshed in a doping culture currently, and what course of action would best protect and care for current and future cyclists. They would think about how to create the strongest, most robust, and most thriving cycling community now and in the future.

This perspective is also the most likely to consider the short- and long-term well-being of Lance Armstrong as someone with whom cycling has a special relationship: What course of action will nurture him when he is at his lowest point? How should care and empathy for the "dopers" be prioritized in comparison to other concerns?

Considerations that are privileged from an ethics of care perspective are those considerations that impact most on people's well-being, and those considerations that will create the strongest communities over time.

The ethics of care theorist would probably investigate further.

What Would the Virtue Theory Position Be?

Using virtue theory, the UCI's responsibility would be framed in terms of what sort of character the organizational leadership should and should not have on display through their actions, regardless of outcomes achieved through an investigation and what those character traits will provide as a role-model for others.

It may be considered that choosing to proactively work to prevent and stamp out the use of performance-enhancing drugs in sport, that is crack-down on drug cheats, would display the virtues of honesty and integrity that UCI agreed to show when they signed up to the USADA code in the first place. This could enhance the credibility of the people involved, the organization, and the sport. The virtue theorist could argue that this reputation is the foundation of trust in the sport and each person involved or engaged with cycling has at some point trusted that they will be involved (as a participant or viewer) with fair competition between elite athletes.

The UCI's responsibility in this respect might be seen as: To be who they say they are going to be and to display the virtues of both sports people and leaders. They might prefer to act well in the face of such complex challenges over other considerations, such as what might happen next or what might be the cost and to whom.

The virtue theorist would probably investigate further.

There is obviously not an easy or even ideal outcome to a situation as complex as this. The dilemma is a useful one to look at for this very reason, as it has layers of implications all around and touches on all of "the classics" that we mentioned earlier: truth versus loyalty, long-term versus short-term outcomes, individual versus community, and justice versus mercy. As you can see, however, the use of theory lets you get much closer to the best-case resolutions that make sense to you, that you can live with, and importantly, that you can explain to other people.

When there is a lack of literacy on ethics and ethical theory, it is harder to "read the play" on people's intentions and motivations as well as we might, and harder to explain our own ethical positions well without seeming narrow, unconcerned, or even hypocritical.

Many leaders, who think that they are describing their ethical positions, are completely missing the mark for parts of their audience. As we explored in the room full of dilemma-busters, consequences might not rank as important at all for some people, and so when they listen to a leader talking about outcomes that are at risk or what might be lost, what they hear is a whole bunch of stuff that does not speak to what they value or what they think is right: "All you talk about is consequences! No mention of character, no mention of duty—you just care about results!" Alternatively, if the leader describes a position and doesn't make mention of consequences, part of his or her audience is likely to be thinking: "What a joke! Talking about character in the face of a crisis, so impractical!" And then there may be others who bemoan the leader who is so busy with being rational and sticking to the policy and commitments, that they have forgotten to pay attention to the people who will be affected by the choices and actions. It is incredibly important to pay attention to the various voices in the conversation, the various interests of people, and to speak to those interests, if you want your actions to be understood as ethical.

People in power in sport need to make choices like these all the time, and they need to give voice to their values, perspectives, and reservations in a confident and composed manner. When leaders give voice to their values, their voice becomes part of the story and a force for change. Without such action, all the awareness and theory in the world still risks being moot and silence can still bring us unstuck.

Check-Out

Ethics does not need to be tribal. There are some options that we have in life that may be actually perfectly consistent with duty, and be virtuous, and have good consequences, and clearly if you have all of those things in one available choice, you have a very powerful option to pursue.

Each theory has some appeal, and this is why the ENDgame framework draws from each to facilitate your thinking. It is not necessary to agree with each element in a theory, nor is it necessary to agree with only one theory. The fact is that no ethical system or principle is going to work all the time.

The point of ethics is to do the right thing, not to construct the perfect formula for doing the right thing. It is not only acceptable, it is necessary to use a variety of ethical approaches to solve certain problems. In real life rather than in theory, situations come up that just don't fit neatly into an existing box.

The need to look like we are unambiguous, in control and in charge or the fear of being embarrassed may sometimes stop us from raising an idea, an alternative position, or a problem. Yet, when a leader is able to park his or her pride, and ask "what can we do next?" not as a test, but as an openly vulnerable request for input it provides the opportunity to lead the solution collaboratively. A coach or a CEO saying "I don't know what to do here" can be an extraordinarily motivating and freeing thing for others to hear.

- Values and principles alone don't always offer the answer to ethical dilemmas; Theory can anchor your thinking down when this happens and let you explore more deeply your options, your commitments, and promises, the consequences you think are most likely with each choice, and importantly, what you think you can live with.
- The major "families of thought" look at the right thing to do from the perspective of consequences (outcomes), duties, and obligations, and whether the behavior was "virtuous" or not. This can radically alter your take on whether something is "good and right" as an action.
- It is unlikely that one doctrine will meet all your needs all of the time, so don't feel that you have to buy-in to one, wholesale; the idea is to use concepts and questions from the big ideas to help you analyze your thinking and work through to good decisions. You can mix it up!

The next chapter gives us a more up-close-and-personal look at the things that go wrong and how to avoid them.

CHAPTER 4

What You Might See at the Top of the "Slippery Slope"

Check-In

You have probably heard the expressions the "slippery slope" and the "thin end of the wedge," which suggest that a relatively small first step can lead to a chain of related events that can end up having a much more significant impact. The expressions are often used in relation to giving small concessions or permissions that are seemingly innocuous, but that may open the door to larger and clearly undesirable actions that were never the intention of the person, who gave the concession or permission.

The expressions are also apt for describing the constant derailing of ethical behavior by the misuse of principles such as the Golden Rule ("do unto others as you would have done to you," which becomes "if it wouldn't trouble me it shouldn't trouble you," for example).

Sometimes, such misuses are honest misconceptions. But there are many examples of convenient and intentional distortions of ethical principles too.

There are also some fine examples of rationalizations and justifications for unethical actions that are simply self-serving excuses for not doing the right thing or not doing anything at all.

And then there are straight-up myths. These are the positions that people take to explain their actions that just don't make any sense. Great creativity, but complete nonsense ethically!

We are going to take a look at a range of typical and common examples of excuses throughout the next two chapters with a view to helping you detect them before they become traps which you walk in to and which can send you and your organization heading down the slippery slope.

Even as I write this, I cringe in recognition of traps I have walked into myself over time or things I have let slide in the behavior of others and not acted on. You may feel something similar. I want to reiterate here that lots of good, decent people make errors of judgment ethically. If we were talking about another part of your leadership practice, perhaps something you already view in terms of being a necessary competency (such as managing people, commercial acumen, or strategic thinking), the learning curve might feel more comfortable. Because ethics involves questions of character and social acceptability, it can be harder on the ego.

Stick with it. To quote Will Durant, "education is a progressive discovery of our own ignorance."[1]

Why Does This Matter?

If you are in professional or semiprofessional sports in a sports-loving nation, your organization and, by extension you, are probably in the public eye for at least some of the time.

Add to this the fact that what you do as a leader in sport, particularly your mistakes, will be likely to make it to the news reel, print media, and Twittersphere even when those mistakes appear to have no material impact on anyone outside of your organization. It is a strong recipe for handling things in-house and sticking with what you know.

Sport is replete with people who are seen as heroes. This can sometimes extend to you as a leader, but even if not, it will likely extend to some of the people who you work with, for, or on behalf of. Being a hero means that you are supposed to be inimitable—surpassing all others, matchless—worse still, perfect! Because elite sport is overglamorized, people make all sorts of assumptions about the magical capabilities or deviant, villainous personalities of people associated with it. If you are seen as a hero, villain, or even a plain old role model, this might make it just a little bit harder to be vulnerable and unsure, to raise your hand and say "I don't know what I should do here," particularly on questions of ethics or questions of character. The reluctance may be part ego, part embarrassment, and partly a lack of knowing what to do next.

The problem with this reluctance is that you end up with the status quo, and we're looking for progress.

This is an opportunity to quietly see what you recognize, what you reject, and what you already stand firmly against in your own attitudes, beliefs, and habits.

It is easy to dismiss white lies, shortcuts, lazy mistakes you can't be bothered to address as careless slips of the tongue, or as small and insignificant, especially when you have a big and important agenda, and not least when you think that bigger agenda is a "good and right" one. But the little wrongs along the way often involve harm and needless risk. Even if you get away with them, they are hazardous to your organizational culture, corroding the values and behaviors that you have probably said matter to you, publicly. Eventually the truth that your stated values are malleable, inconsistent, or fickle becomes the unspoken thing that your team knows. At that point, you give people very little to trust and rely on in you as the leader when it comes to ethics. On culture and ethics, you do sometimes need to sweat the small stuff.

Discussion

One of the ways to conceive of the kind of early warning signs of attitudes, habits, and embedded excuses that can start you on the slippery slope to ethical issues, is to think of them as "traps" to be noticed, stepped around, and avoided where possible. Independently, each trap may not amount to anything too serious. But unchecked and normalized, these are the kind of habitual excuses for poor conduct that put organizations at cultural risk of much larger issues creeping up.

The following traps are referenced and informed in large part from the ethicsalarms.com rulebook and adapted for the sporting context.[2]

Misconceptions, Myths, Distortions, Justifications, Rationalizations, and Other High-Risk Excuses

"Free-Speech" Trap

The fact that we enjoy free speech in Western societies means people are at liberty to express an opinion, make a comment, or criticize someone or something in the public domain. This right is considered so important to our political freedom that it is articulated in both the United Nations Declaration of Human Rights as well as the International Covenant on Civil and Political rights. However, this right does not equate to an immediate moral right to speak recklessly, dishonestly, or to insult and vilify others.

"It is my right to say what I want" is often invoked as a misuse of a principle in sport when it comes to issues of discrimination. Being afforded the right to free speech does not also afford someone the right to scream obscenities and abuse from the sidelines. Neither does it mean that behind closed doors in the boardroom or locker-room it is OK to express hateful sentiments that denigrate and disrespect other people on the basis of race, gender, sexual orientation, or disability. It doesn't make it any more moral if things are said in private. The reason this moves into ethical territory is because it is injurious in nature; it hurts people. You may be free to say it, but that doesn't necessarily mean it is right.

"Tit for Tat" Trap

This one is a misuse of the "eye for an eye" principle, one interpretation of which is that the "victim" of some misdemeanor is deserving of the "equivalent value" of their own "injury" in compensation. In the unethical contortion of this principle it seems that if a person acts unethically in response to someone else doing so first, somehow it is OK; you have an unethical "free-kick" so to speak. However, not only do two wrongs not make a right but no wrong that another person did extends you leeway on what wrong you can do; it is not hard to see a pretty quick path down the slippery slope of abandoned values here. Mahatma Gandhi put it best when he said, "an eye for an eye makes everyone blind."[3]

"Righteous" Traps

Regardless of your religious persuasion (or lack thereof), you are probably familiar with everyday rationalization for *not* acting, that resort to religious text for support: "Judge not, lest ye not be judged," and "Let him who is without sin cast the first stone" are examples (Matthew 7:1; John 8: 7,10,11). Both quotes are distorted and misused as a defense for unethical behavior.

"Judge not, lest ye not be judged " is frequently cited to support the position that it is inherently wrong to judge the conduct of others. However, the practice of ethical leadership involves the observation, analysis, and judgment of behaviors in oneself and in others. This is the way ethical standards are established, normalized, and maintained in society, and societal standards are less likely to be upheld if people choose to bail out when it comes to taking a position on the tricky stuff. The sentiment of the "judge not, lest you be judged" quote is intended to *clarify* ethical standards rather than undermine them. It means that you should be willing to be judged by the same standards you expect of others, and that you can judge someone's behavior without considering them a bad person, a fool, or someone inherently immoral. In fact, you can still like a person who, in your judgment, has done the wrong thing!

The second rationalization in this realm, "let him who is without sin cast the first stone" is frequently used to support the contention that only those who are perfect, with no past infringements at all, no slip ups or black marks, are qualified to judge the behavior of others. This one strays particularly far from its original meaning when it is distorted and used to avoid acting ethically. In origin it was a tale about redemption, a caution against hypocrisy, and a reminder that we are all held to the same account.

"It Was Just One Mistake" Trap

This is the excuse that a particular unethical act should be ignored, forgiven, or excused because "it was just one mistake." There are two main problems with this. The first is that the mistake might be grave enough in nature that it doesn't matter if the person has never received a penalty or send-off since starting junior sport; it is still blatantly unethical and harmful *independent* of whatever has gone before.

The second is that the just one mistake clause can be used dishonestly and deceptively to distract attention from the fact that the "act" was probably not an aberration, a one-off impulse, but more likely the result of a series of choices requiring judgment along the way.

In the 2009 "Bloodgate" affair involving English Rugby Club Harlequins, the side used fake blood capsules to facilitate a tactical substitution. Harlequins were considered a "Proud old club dragged into the gutter" by coach Dean Richards when he ordered the act.[4] Richards was considered to have had a brain-fade around Bloodgate, not befitting of a man who was so passionate about his club and talented at his job. It was just one mistake.

The reality is that the problem was not the incident on April 12, 2009 (considered one of the most scandalous in rugby union since professionalization in the mid 1990s), which made the case so unethical. It was the continuous stream of small judgments and decisions over years across governance, football operations, medical, coaching, and athletes involving lies, cover-ups, deceit, self-interest, and betrayal that permitted an incident to be even possible where a player bit a fake blood capsule, the coaches called the sub, and then the club doctor actually cut the players lip to try and cover up the lie once detection seemed imminent.

"Nobody Is Perfect" Trap

Indeed, nobody is perfect. Perfect is a myth in itself. However, when "nobody is perfect" is used as a defense, it is often an attempt to minimize the significance of genuine misconduct. The fact that nobody is perfect does not mean that it isn't necessary and appropriate to point out unethical conduct when it occurs, or to strive to make sure it doesn't happen again. Likewise, we do all make mistakes but to use that as a reason to avoid addressing unethical conduct makes no sense. We are all still accountable for the mistakes we make. The fact of imperfection is pretty much irrelevant to the act in question (although you may choose to account for this view of human nature in the way you handle an ethical mistake with compassion).

"Take Life Too Seriously" Trap

This one is designed to minimize unethical conduct by dismissing it as just a bit of fun, casual banter, or light-hearted humor. A common retort to ethical issues being pointed out, particularly around things that people have said that offended or shamed others, is to decry political correctness and lament that everyone takes life too seriously these days. To reiterate an earlier point, we get into ethical territory where there is the potential for harm, and when there is a dimension of genuine rightness or wrongness to an action. Humor often involves some irreverence, but there is a big difference between being "cheeky" and showing deep disrespect and contempt that normalize hatred, exclusion, and discrimination. Light-hearted humor can be either of these.

"What Will Be Next" Trap

This is where sarcasm and even a degree of irreverence are used in an attempt to make the original, legitimate point seem unreasonable, by raising related but absurd variations of things that one might have to do next in the name of doing the right thing that are unreasonable beyond doubt. For example, "Now we are being lobbied to take out the leg slide to protect players! What's next, a complete body-armor of bubble wrap for the lower body? Feather cushioned shin pads and cotton wool socks?" This end of the world type overreach is designed to diffuse tension and to make people uncomfortable enough not to continue to push on the conduct, or responsibilities in question.

"No-Choice" Trap

This myth is when people say they had to behave unethically because they had no choice. There may of course be life-and-death situations where this is true but not in sport. As we noted earlier, part of behaving ethically is about being willing to accept the cost of your choices. In some cases people feel the cost is too high or requires too much personal sacrifice, courage, shame, criticism, risk, loss, or pain to act ethically. The fact is that there was still a choice. You may not have liked the choices you had, but you are still accountable for the choice you made. Creating a myth of coercion simply moves moral responsibility away from you.

When a rookie athlete says she had no choice but to use a banned substance in her sport because her coach said she must or he would not be able to select her, the excuse is just that, an excuse. We might feel sympathy recognizing the coach's abuse of his power to meet his own needs, but there was a choice and in this case the athlete valued selection more than she valued not cheating. Similarly, the sport organization, for example, that claims to have no choice in continuing a commercial relationship with a provider that has proven unethical in the past through deceit, fraud, monopolizing, or price fixing, because the market is too tight or there is no time or there is no decent alternative, simply is not prepared to accept the cost of choosing not to work with the provider. The value placed on commercial return and achieving targets is greater than the value placed on fair-trading.

"Victim's Leeway" Trap

When someone belongs to a group that is commonly treated with bias, or has a history of being so (such as some minority groups), or when an individual feels, perhaps legitimately, that he or she is personally discriminated against or disliked because of external factors such as appearance, social background, past indiscretions, or perceived personality problems, the "victim mindset" can mean that the person may refuse to acknowledge their own wrongdoing or mistakes, choosing instead to rationalize and view the criticism as unfair discrimination ("you wouldn't take issue with me as a coach for having an affair with a junior athlete if I were a man"). Someone may be biased against you but still be right in their assessment of your misconduct.

"No Harm, No Foul" Trap

One of the great criticisms of consequentialism (explored in chapter 3 as ethical egoism and utilitarianism) is that it potentially ignores how you get to the outcome you want; even cruel, damaging, and illegal conduct is supposed to be ethical because good consequences resulted, or no serious harm was done in the end. This trap encapsulates the idea that even though technically a breach of a code or a law may have occurred, there is no need for punishment, apology, or retribution as no actual damage resulted. This excuse can be used to justify discriminatory behavior in sport; "He wasn't particularly offended by the racial slur so what's the problem?" or "her performance wasn't actually improved by the drug so no harm was done."

"It Was for a Good Cause" Trap

This one is an end-justifies-the-means rationalization for behaving badly in pursuit of an outcome that is seen as a good thing. Often though the action taken has been covert, unspoken, or covered up in some way and the desired outcome, or "good cause" is self-serving.

A classic example of this was the stolen medical records case in Australian Rules Football (AFL) in 2007. A journalist was found to have bought the medical records of AFL players from two individuals who had reportedly found them in a gutter opposite a medical clinic (and later pleaded guilty to "theft by finding"). The records were purported to indicate that the players had used illicit drugs. The defense was that the moral imperative to tell the story and out the players was for the best and done to protect the sport from drugs. Buying private medical records was wrong, and the fact that you did not actually steal them, or that they were found in a gutter, does not alter the gross violation of privacy or the gravity of the act, even though it allowed the journalist to break a story he believed was for the common good.

"The King's Pass" Trap

This dangerous justification presumes that the special status of a person, as a celebrity or leader, powerbroker, or superstar high achiever somehow earns them a more lenient ethical standard. This free-pass is awarded on the basis that either the person is too important or too special to "trouble" with concerns on personal moral standard, or that the person has some sort of ethical credit in the bank because he or she has achieved a lot in life, making him or her untouchable as in our media leak example earlier.

A classic sports example of this is the all-powerful president, chairperson, or owner of a sports club getting away with bullying behavior, or social misconduct that would be admonished in a more junior staff member, or the lack of action on the conduct of a very influential patron or donor who nobody is keen to get offside, because there is too much to lose.

"Ethics Accounting" Trap

You cannot earn the right to act unethically by depositing a lot of ethical deeds in the imaginary ethics bank, nor can an unethical conduct be erased or balanced out by doing something good after the event. Unethical conduct is unethical conduct, whatever went before or after. There is an unsavory habit in elite sport of using charity and community work as penance for misconduct, which suggests first that such work is a punishing chore, and also that you can make up for the domestic violence incident or drunken public brawl resulting in criminal charges or bet you placed on your own game and so on with a good deed. This is neither educational nor useful in any way in terms of developing better ethical decision making in future, although it may improve your public brand marginally, with the not-yet-cynical and for the short term.

"Stupid Rule Anyway" Trap

This one justifies an unethical action by demeaning the rule or standard that got in the way of you doing what you wanted, or caught you out. This suggests that you can decide yourself which rules and standards to violate depending on what *you* deem intelligent and reasonable. This is likely to also be convenient and self-serving. No doubt some rules seem arbitrary and unnecessary, but circumventing them consciously puts your own authority higher than the collective body that brought the rule or standard to bear—probably the experts.

"If it Isn't Illegal" Trap

The law is clearly a guide for right and wrong behavior, one that is externally applied and enforced. However, it is not enough to inhibit all forms of poor conduct or harmful behavior. A code for ethical conduct, while also a guide for right and wrong behavior, is self-motivated, based on the individual's values and the internalized desire to do the right thing. The two need to work alongside. All that happens when people say that "if it isn't illegal it must be OK" is a complete shifting of responsibility, to someone or something other than the self to make choices about how to live.

There is much that is unethical that is not illegal: Take the examples of favoritism and cronyism seen so regularly in sport, where a person is offered opportunity not because they are the best or most suited, but because they belong to a group of friends and associates, old school boys, or ex-team mates ("it's not what you know, it's who you know"). Favoritism and cronyism interfere with fairness and transparency (and often equal opportunity), but they are not necessarily illegal.

"Everybody Does it" Trap

This rationalization is based on the assumption that the recourse due or response to unethical acts should be less, because there are many examples of other people doing it too. Using this rationalization, most people are actually acknowledging that they know right from wrong and are behaving poorly. However, the claim is that they shouldn't be singled out for condemnation because everybody else is doing it too and that wouldn't be fair.

The "bounty-gate" scandal in National Football League (NFL) in 2011 saw elements of this play out in the initial defense offered by New Orleans Saints for a scheme that saw players being paid a bounty for intentionally injuring opposition players so badly that they were taken out of the game. The twin arguments that "football is a tough game, anyone who goes out there knows they can get hurt" and, "everyone incentivizes" in some way, many other teams do this "kind of thing" ran in defense of the bounty scheme. Both arguments actually acknowledge intentional harm. The first argument ignores what it is that players consent to when they go out there, which is sanctioned contact, not intentional injury, and the second argument attempts to dilute the significance of the misconduct by demonstrating similar kinds of (legal and illegal) incentivization elsewhere ("they are just as bad").

The "it's been going on for years/just the way it is" defense is in a similar category of excuse, and not much more than an attempt at distraction from unethical behavior.

"He's One of the Good Guys" Trap

"He/she is a great person" is a rationalization in which the act is judged by the perceived goodness of the person doing it, rather than the other way around. If a person is held in such high regard and indeed if a person has such conviction that they are of good character themselves (supported by their experiences), it can seem almost outlandish that they might do something ethically wrong. They might be almost *above suspicion.* Yet complacency, laziness, environments, peer pressure, performance pressure, and corrupted leadership can influence our choices on a daily basis. Nobody who suffers from the human condition is above the possibility of ethical misconduct.

The challenge, when a good person does a bad thing, is that we don't want to acknowledge the disappointment of it, and there can be a diminished urge to penalize or sanction the behavior. Nobody wants to *shoot Bambi.*

"If I Don't Do It Someone Else Will" Trap

This rationalization diminishes the need for doing the right thing because the wrong thing is certain to occur anyway. If you believe that the outcome is inevitable, why not get ahead of the curve? This rationalization has been used to excuse talent scouts and recruiters from negotiations and enticements with underage players not yet eligible for draft, sports journalists breaking unfounded and damaging stories in lieu of all the facts, and those involved in match fixing, price fixing, cheating, monopolizing, and saturating sports markets with gambling and alcohol advertisements among many other things.

The idea that an ethical refusal to partake will only cause the abstainer pain and not prevent any damage anyway is self-serving logic. Sometimes it will make a difference, and sometimes the example of a leader is a powerful one.

"It's Not My Fault" Trap

This rationalization suggests that we are each only responsible for responding ethically to problems that we personally created; "If I didn't create it, bad luck, not my problem." Two on-field examples illustrate the point here.

In the 2013 FA cup soccer season, Uruguayan striker Luis Suarez (Liverpool Football club) illegally handled the ball on the way into the net for a winning goal against Mansfield. The crowd saw it, the TV cameras caught it, the Mansfield players saw it, and only Luis Suarez will ever know if it was intent, instinct, or misfortune that led him to handle the ball. The fact that the referee did not see it and disallow the goal was "not Suarez's fault." However, he did have a choice to tell the referee, or not lie if questioned. This would have been "just" an act of sportsmanship that may have made no material difference if the referee maintained his decision. However, it is an excellent example of the normalized slippery slope of excuses, blame shifting, denial, and exoneration of responsibility common in sport.

The second example is Australian cricketer Adam Gilchrist's famous "walk" when he was caught out in the 2003 cricket World Cup semi-final against Sri Lanka. The umpire ruled not out, but Gilchrist ignored the ruling knowing it to be incorrect and left the field.

The following excerpt from his book describes the moment of choice:

> Then, to see the umpire shaking his head, meaning, "Not out," gave me the strangest feeling. I don't recall what my exact thoughts were, but somewhere in the back of my mind, all that history from the Ashes series was swirling around. Michael Vaughan, Nasser Hussain and the other batsmen, both in my team and against us, who had stood their ground in those "close" catching incidents were definitely a factor in what happened in the following seconds. I had spent all summer wondering if it was possible to take ownership of these incidents and still be successful. I had wondered what I would do. I was about to find out.
>
> The voice in my head was emphatic. Go. Walk.
>
> And I did.[5]

Gilchrist goes on to describe how much doubt he experienced after the decision, not least in the face of a divided cricket community. Despite Australia winning the match, there was a "cost" for his actions. Some chided Gilchrist as disloyal and even foolish. It was not his fault the umpire got it wrong, but he "chose" to live his values and walk.

"There Are Worse Things" Trap

This is a ludicrous rationalization for misconduct. For most ethical misconduct in sport, there are certainly worse things, but the benchmarks are ideals of good behavior, not the bad behavior of others. Somebody else's worse thing has no true bearing on your conduct at all. The only reason to consider the precedent set by others is if you are on a tribunal of some kind handing out penalties.

"Boys Will Be Boys" Trap

This is a popular rationalization for ethical issues arising usually with groups of men and often involving sexual misconduct, fighting, and abuse of alcohol or other drugs. It suggests that there is somehow a biological or gendered impediment to acting ethically; that being a *boy* (the term is often used to refer to men in their twenties or even thirties) means you are less able to show self-control, have no ability to deny or resist desires, and thus are excused for acting according to impulse. Not only does this dumb men down, it creates a tone of acceptance of questionable behavior.

There are many examples of team-bonding sessions across many sports that have resulted in serious sexual misconduct. The sexual objectification and degradation of women has been theorized as being a way to forge closeness, assert power and hyper-masculinity, and deepen a shared identity.

This form of bonding was highlighted in the Australian National Rugby League sex scandals in 2009 that uncovered the practice of players passing around one woman in group-sex sessions, some of which were apparently consensual and some of which were allegedly gang-rape. In defense of the practice, some commentators shifted blame to the women involved and rationalized that if the women were consenting, and put themselves in such a situation, the boys' responsibility for what happened next was questionable.

Descriptions of "boys just bonding" and "letting off steam" dilute the significance of moral choices and represent silent complicity in poor behavior such as sexism or sexual violence.

"These Are Not Ordinary Times" Trap

This rationalization suggests that standards, values, and ethical conduct are adjustable, and can and should be suspended under special circumstances. These circumstances can include pressures such as financial constraints and competing strategic imperatives, or they can be about the window of opportunity to win that is presenting right now and must not be obscured by distractions like acting ethically or responding to issues around culture and leadership. This position says "standards and values are fine and good but not right now, I'm busy."

In reality, times of intensified pressure may lead to emotional volatility and higher risk of straying from your values. It is a critical time to be focused on standards of ethical leadership. Rationalizing "special times" simply creates a convenient "opt-out" possibility.

"It's for His Own Good" Trap

This justification is sometimes given for bullying, suggesting that there is an ultimate, benevolent motive for harassing, abusing, and humiliating people, especially young people or people in subordinate power positions in the workplace. While sport may be seen to play a role in developing character, all bullying does is to reign down damage and create more bullies with no idea how to challenge in respectful ways. The same applies in the offices, boardrooms, and locker rooms that house sports leaders.

Old school, tough, aggressive leaders may have made their mark on you as leaders and been abusive along the way. To reiterate my earlier point, it is entirely possible to like someone whose conduct is out of line. You have a choice to lead *your way*. It is possible to be both hard and strong whilst not losing your ethical compass.

The oft-used sports adage "only pressure makes a diamond" is designed to be a reference to the pressure one faces when rising to the challenges of being a performer. The sacrifice it takes to achieve great things and the push you might need to get there are arguably for your own good, and that push may include discipline and criticism. But abuse and bullying have no place whatsoever in ethical conduct.

Check-Out

Being able to recognize ethical traps, small and large, is not about catching people out, labeling, or even seeking to blame and punish. It is about putting yourself, as a leader, in a position to lower the risk of culturally normalizing excuses for poor behavior in your organization.

Your job as the leader is to walk toward the risks and issues you see, not turn away from them or hand-ball the responsibility to another authority. It is not easy to do this, because it can feel risky; not everyone is comfortable positioning themselves as a moral authority and potentially being seen as a *wowzer*, being ridiculed, thwarted, or dismissed as self-important. Perhaps it seems easier on the surface to broker quiet deals, shirk higher authority, or manipulate outcomes behind the scenes and avoid using your voice out loud. You might even thumb your nose at "the official position" and quietly sympathize with the dissent—if so, ask yourself what is in it for you to do this? Do you really believe it? Or does it maintain your informal power and safety? Are you valuing your comfort more than your leadership? It is harder to earn genuine respect and support this way even if you stay in the "in group," and it is hard to model strong leadership in secret.

A way forward is to start working out how to say what you actually would prefer to say. It is not necessary to always stand at the front of a group and call out the slippery slope trap or excuse that you see, and on many occasions there is a more effective, subtle way to address things. However, an ethical leader does need to have the courage of his or her convictions. If you find yourself wanting someone else to make the hard calls and act on them, it might be time to revisit the methods and approaches you are using to voice your values everyday rather than wait for something to go really wrong. I address this more fully in Chapter 6.

Very few people leave the house in the morning intending to do the wrong thing. Neither do they intend grand moments of moral fortitude. The reality is that a sound ethical practice in an organization is created by "small ethics" as much as big tests.

- While rationalizations for action (or inaction) on misconduct come in many forms, they are all really just self-serving excuses offered for choosing not to do the right thing. This may be intentional or unintentional, but the result is the same.
- Almost all of the traps explored here consider behavior that is "at someone else's expense," again highlighting the centrality of the quality of relationships we have with others when it comes to acting ethically.
- The most common thread across the traps is harm. It gets ethically messy whenever a person is put in harm's way (physically, emotionally, psychologically, materially, or in terms of reputation) by your action or inaction on moral standards.
- It is not just the enormous ethical failings (the ones that leave people shaking their heads and saying "what were they thinking?") that you need to look out for. The big ones are sometimes a shock, but you may also be able to see them coming long before they materialize if you look with "soft eyes"—in a way that takes in the whole cultural picture—rather than "hard eyes" that focuses just on outcomes and

problems. It is important to continue to ask "what is the ethical content I can see here?"; it is one of the habits that will serve you best as an ethical leader.

You have a lot of background information—time now to put it into practice.

CHAPTER 5
A Case Study

Check-In

This chapter gives you an active opportunity to apply the "ENDgame" ethical decision-making framework to a contemporary case study in sport.

I cannot emphasize enough the importance of getting into new habits rather than just relying on what you've done before when it comes to living your values in sport. The framework is a guide to create such a habit; not a watertight system for getting everything right or a fail-proof model for integrity in sport, but a guide for applying your ethical intelligence, so that the chances of reaching an ethical decision are higher and the risks of making unethical decisions are lower.

The case is presented to you *as if* you were an organizational leader charged with acting on behalf of the sport in question.

Using any framework or model can be initially cumbersome and feel overanalytical. In reality, many of your ethical decisions are made quickly, under time pressure and on the go. It may be that you think "I never have time to go through each decision in this much detail!", that's OK; it's a process of learning and habituation. Like the development of many skills, initially it may take you a lot longer than the way you were doing it that had served you well enough up until now. Eventually though, it becomes a learned process once again and you get to operate at a much higher level as an ethical leader.

It is also a reality that in many cases we choose options that we think are possible, rather than ideal. As mentioned earlier, the idea is to act as best as we can in the given circumstances, not to create a perfect formula, or a textbook decision that doesn't actually work practically. Because we predict what we think is possible, the decision-making process isn't linear; we don't truly work things out step-by-step: We jump ahead, revisit the last insight when we get a new one, and sometimes feel like you know where you are going to end up by the end of the E in ENDgame. There is no problem with this, remember the model is just a container for information and a guide for thinking.

At the completion of this chapter you should have a fairly good understanding of how to arrive at a decision having worked through a sound process of ethical reflection. This means you will more than likely be able to work out what you think is the right thing to do and whether the choice sits well with you.

Discussion

The context for this example is a recent ethical debate in sport based around an accusation of racism between elite golfers that escalated into the public domain and resulted in calls for leadership action from within the community both on the incident itself and on institutionalized racism within the sport.

The example presents an opportunity to reflect on the job of the leader in sport, as well as the values and principles that sport represents, and how they might come in to conflict at times.

Case Study: Racism and Golf

In May 2013, Spanish golfer Sergio Garcia found himself under fire in the media after an ill-informed and allegedly "off-the-cuff" comment about "serving fried chicken" to the black American golfer, Tiger Woods. The jibe was widely interpreted as racist. Garcia has subsequently apologized profusely to Woods and to the community at large, but remains convinced that his comment was *not intended* to be racist. The community remains divided about whether it is possible to be "accidentally racist" and whether sport has a duty to act on social justice issues such as this as role models, or whether the media response is overblown and sensationalized.

The leadership of golf is now under pressure to react decisively to Garcia's *joke* if they are serious about their commitment to changing the sport from being a mostly white domain to a more inclusive multicultural environment.

As the Sergio Garcia and Tiger Woods racism row escalates, the following questions arise:

- *How should golf's leadership respond to the incident overall? What is their primary job and how would their actions reflect their sporting vision?*
- *How should golf's leadership respond to Garcia and why?*
- *What are sports' values and how should it order these values?*

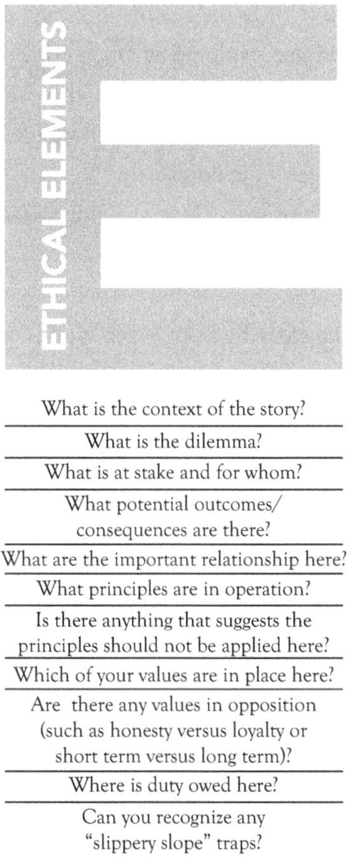

Figure 5.1 "E" of ENDgame framework

A decision on how to proceed most ethically on this case takes a fair degree of analysis and reflection, remembering that there is rarely a perfect scenario for all stakeholders. I am going to ask you to approach this case study as if you were part of a senior leadership group for the International Golf Federation (IGF), and your task at hand is to work out what *you believe* will be the right things to do using the ENDgame framework as a guide.

On your first read through of the media report of the following situation, look for what general ethical content you can see in the report. This is the "E" in the ENDgame framework presented here in Figure 5.1, but you can refer back to chapter 2 on dilemmas, values, virtues, morals, and principles if you need a refresher.

Try to suspend your early judgment on blame or a course of action until you have clarified and explored as much ethical content as possible. Even though you will likely predict ahead, this way you might be less tempted to make your answers fit your first judgment and you can work through it openly and see what comes up.

First, consider how this story (facts and impressions) can be seen from various angles:

- What might the story be from Tiger Woods' point of view?
- What about from Sergio Garcia's point of view?
- How do you see your responsibility as the governing body?
- Stretch your imagination to consider all reasonable consequences or potential outcomes that you can envisage:
    - What could this mean for sponsors?
    - Tour organizers?
    - For other golfers in this tournament and elsewhere?
    - What about for media representatives?
    - Public relations?
    - What about for community program managers working on multicultural engagement initiatives?

Perhaps take a moment to write down your initial thoughts, after reading the following report, before reviewing some possibilities that I have highlighted as examples in the next section (in Figure 5.2).

The Independent
Thursday 23rd May 2013

The joke wasn't funny any more. It never was, of course, and the sense of revulsion felt by all in golf weighed heavily on Sergio Garcia. A throwaway line dressed up as banter had become a stain on Garcia's character that might never wash away. The talk should have been about golf, a celebration of the stellar talent on show over the next four days at the European Tour's flagship event. Instead Wentworth reeled beneath a racist pall cast by Garcia's ill-judged insult aimed at Tiger Woods.

The sarcastic offer to cook fried chicken for golf's ethnic totem not only pointed to a tolerance of casual racism in the individual, it did nothing to counter the deeply held prejudice that golf is a sport only for middle-class white folk. A sweep of Wentworth's polished lawns reveals precious few black faces. The field of 153 is overwhelmingly white, peppered only by the odd entry from Asia.

Golf is open to all but not all choose to take up the offer, which ought to be a concern for the game's stakeholders, who on days like this are open to the barb that they care more about the mechanics of the putting stroke than the exclusive demography of its constituents.

Garcia was suitably contrite, and as far as anyone can tell, sincere in his apology. He said sorry to the European Tour, his fellow professionals and, most importantly, to Woods, with whom he shares a rivalry that has never been anything but sour, and which lately turned toxic. But this was different.

Garcia's remark expressed not outrage at a perceived slight but a dangerous and abhorrent attitude toward a competitor based on race. This is a territory from which golf has galloped at a furious rate, yet without ever convincing the black community that sport is a game for them, too. Garcia understood the gravity of his position, claiming that it had kept him awake most of the night and prompted him to consider withdrawal from the BMW PGA Championship.

"As soon as I left the dinner I started to get a sick feeling in my body," he said. "I wasn't able to sleep at all. I felt like my heart was going to come out of my body and I've had a sick feeling all day. It has been difficult to hit a shot without thinking about it. Unfortunately I said it. The only thing I can do is say sorry."

It was hoped that Woods might be the great stereotype-buster to break a taboo that had lingered far too long. The idea that golf was a pastime for middle-class elites was historically reinforced by a divided society split overtly along racial lines. The race bar was lifted at America's most famous club, Augusta National, only 23 years ago when it admitted its first black member. But the county club scene remains predominantly a white domain.

Woods was first caught in the racist undertow after his record-breaking victory at the Masters in 1997 when Fuzzy Zoeller infamously advised: "You pat him on the back and say congratulations and enjoy it and tell him not to serve fried chicken next year. Got it? Or collard greens or whatever the hell they serve."

In November 2011, caddie Steve Williams triggered another racist controversy, referring to Woods as a black arsehole in what he thought was light-hearted banter. Both Zoeller and Williams apologised. Neither suffered official sanction but Zoeller was dropped by his sponsors Dunlop and K-Mart.

Garcia is under similar pressure from his sponsors TaylorMade-Adidas, who advised they are monitoring the situation. The European Tour has erred on the side of caution, noting the rapid apology made by Garcia on Tuesday night after he left the stage at the European Tour Awards dinner in London, and the more profound contrition. While this might be seen as reasonable on material grounds, it could be interpreted as a missed opportunity.

An audience of 500, including sponsors and other golf high rollers, winced during the interview conducted on the biggest night of the European Tour calendar. The game preaches inclusion and has extended its boundaries way beyond the European heartland to stay afloat with tournaments throughout Asia and China. It is difficult to see how a tolerance of Garcia's remarks is conducive to the promotion of golf in communities still to be persuaded of its charms.

It looks to outsiders that racism is OK as long as it comes with an apology. Football sees fit to impose an automatic penalty for racist offences. Is it not time for golf to make an example of offenders, however rare the episode, if it is ever to convince the doubters that it is serious about being a sport for all?

Garcia has apologised to Woods but what about the Afro-Caribbean and Afro-American communities? The offence did not stop at Woods' door. It insulted all those who share his ethnicity and have no place in society, let alone golf.

Garcia is among friends today, playing alongside fellow Spaniard Gonzalo Fernandez-Castano and Luke Donald. He hopes his apology will be enough. "Like I said, I was caught off guard by a funny question. I tried to give a funny answer that came out totally wrong. I want to make sure that everybody knows that I'm very, very sorry. I can't apologise enough."

Now golf must ask itself if an apology is enough.[1]

I suspect you have picked up on some good content in this story. In Figure 5.2, I have also highlighted some possible examples of how the ethical content for this story could be seen.

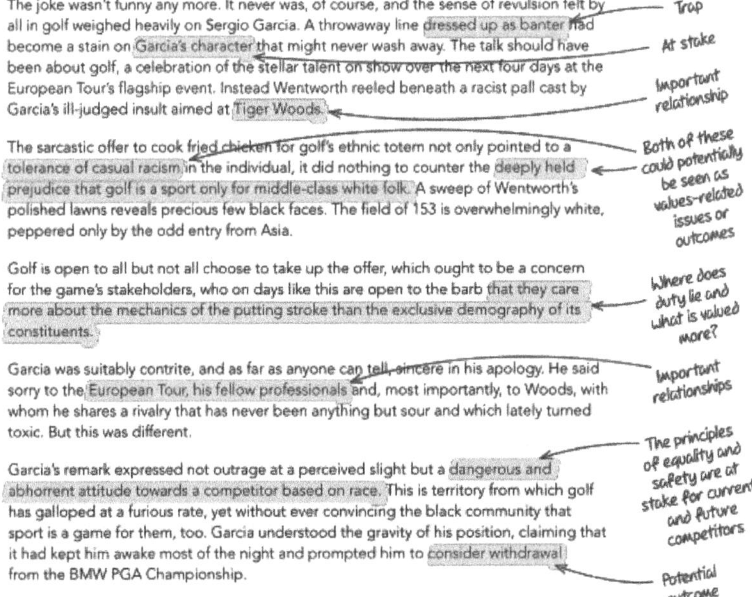

Woods-Garcia racist comment dilemma

The joke wasn't funny any more. It never was, of course, and the sense of revulsion felt by all in golf weighed heavily on Sergio Garcia. A throwaway line dressed up as banter had become a stain on Garcia's character that might never wash away. The talk should have been about golf, a celebration of the stellar talent on show over the next four days at the European Tour's flagship event. Instead Wentworth reeled beneath a racist pall cast by Garcia's ill-judged insult aimed at Tiger Woods.

The sarcastic offer to cook fried chicken for golf's ethnic totem not only pointed to a tolerance of casual racism in the individual, it did nothing to counter the deeply held prejudice that golf is a sport only for middle-class white folk. A sweep of Wentworth's polished lawns reveals precious few black faces. The field of 153 is overwhelmingly white, peppered only by the odd entry from Asia.

Golf is open to all but not all choose to take up the offer, which ought to be a concern for the game's stakeholders, who on days like this are open to the barb that they care more about the mechanics of the putting stroke than the exclusive demography of its constituents.

Garcia was suitably contrite, and as far as anyone can tell, sincere in his apology. He said sorry to the European Tour, his fellow professionals and, most importantly, to Woods, with whom he shares a rivalry that has never been anything but sour and which lately turned toxic. But this was different.

Garcia's remark expressed not outrage at a perceived slight but a dangerous and abhorrent attitude towards a competitor based on race. This is territory from which golf has galloped at a furious rate, yet without ever convincing the black community that sport is a game for them, too. Garcia understood the gravity of his position, claiming that it had kept him awake most of the night and prompted him to consider withdrawal from the BMW PGA Championship.

Figure 5.2 Woods–Garcia racist comment dilemma

As soon as I left the dinner I started to get a sick feeling in my body," he said. "I wasn't able to sleep at all. I felt like my heart was going to come out of my body and I've had a sick feeling all day. It has been difficult to hit a shot without thinking about it. Unfortunately I said it. The only thing I can do is say sorry."

It was hoped that Woods might be the great stereotype-buster to break a taboo that had lingered far too long. The idea that golf was a pastime for middle-class elites was historically reinforced by a divided society split overtly along racial lines. The race bar was lifted at America's most famous club, Augusta National, only 23 years ago when it admitted its first black member. But the county club scene remains predominantly a white domain.

Woods was first caught in the racist undertow after his record-breaking victory at the Masters in 1997 when Fuzzy Zoeller infamously advised: "You pat him on the back and say congratulations and enjoy it and tell him not to serve fried chicken next year. Got it? Or collard greens or whatever the hell they serve."

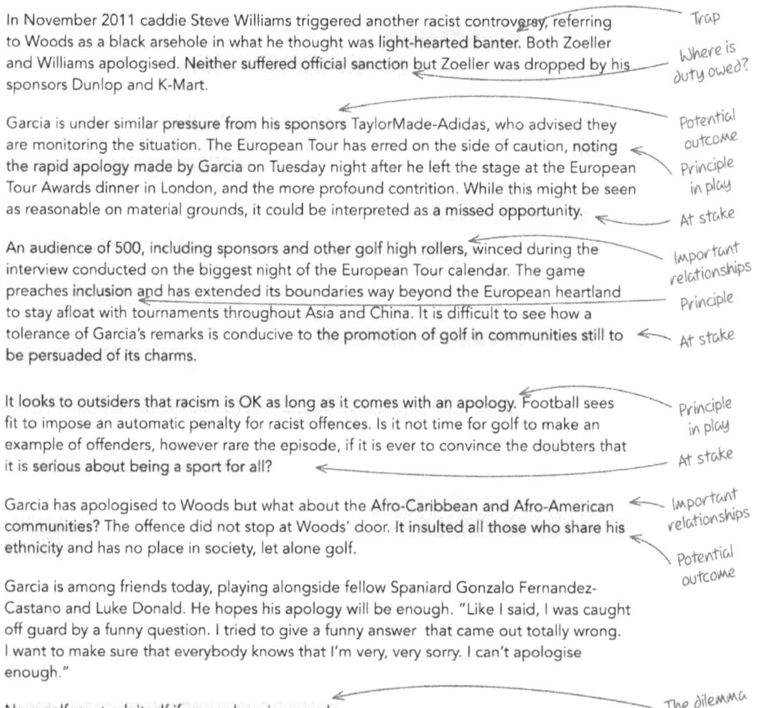

In November 2011 caddie Steve Williams triggered another racist controversy, referring to Woods as a black arsehole in what he thought was light-hearted banter. Both Zoeller and Williams apologised. Neither suffered official sanction but Zoeller was dropped by his sponsors Dunlop and K-Mart.

Garcia is under similar pressure from his sponsors TaylorMade-Adidas, who advised they are monitoring the situation. The European Tour has erred on the side of caution, noting the rapid apology made by Garcia on Tuesday night after he left the stage at the European Tour Awards dinner in London, and the more profound contrition. While this might be seen as reasonable on material grounds, it could be interpreted as a missed opportunity.

An audience of 500, including sponsors and other golf high rollers, winced during the interview conducted on the biggest night of the European Tour calendar. The game preaches inclusion and has extended its boundaries way beyond the European heartland to stay afloat with tournaments throughout Asia and China. It is difficult to see how a tolerance of Garcia's remarks is conducive to the promotion of golf in communities still to be persuaded of its charms.

It looks to outsiders that racism is OK as long as it comes with an apology. Football sees fit to impose an automatic penalty for racist offences. Is it not time for golf to make an example of offenders, however rare the episode, if it is ever to convince the doubters that it is serious about being a sport for all?

Garcia has apologised to Woods but what about the Afro-Caribbean and Afro-American communities? The offence did not stop at Woods' door. It insulted all those who share his ethnicity and has no place in society, let alone golf.

Garcia is among friends today, playing alongside fellow Spaniard Gonzalo Fernandez-Castano and Luke Donald. He hopes his apology will be enough. "Like I said, I was caught off guard by a funny question. I tried to give a funny answer that came out totally wrong. I want to make sure that everybody knows that I'm very, very sorry. I can't apologise enough."

Now golf must ask itself if an apology is enough.

Figure 5.2 (Continued)

At this point it is useful to look back over the story and reflect on the second part of the ENDgame framework, the "N"; the things you **need to notice** in yourself and in your processing of the situation (Figure 5.3).

The type of assumptions you may consider could include an assumption that Sergio Garcia has or has not infringed in this way previously? Or that apology has been accepted by Woods? Or that the

Are you making any assumptions?

Have you done anything to test these assumptions?

Who's responsibility is it to respond to/lead on this issue?

What information is relevant and what should be ignored?

How do you personally feel about the situation and the people involved?

What do you think you would see/feel/experience if you were "in their shoes"?

Are there any hot issues/likely blind spots for you?

***Figure 5.3** "N" of ENDgame framework*

report you have received is accurate? Or perhaps even that there were not a dozen other similar incidents on the tour that made this behavior common place?

Presumably you are not actually in a position to know the facts (and obviously for the sake of the exercise you are working from a media report), but nevertheless it is useful to recognize what information you are developing your understanding with, and to consider what else you might do to round-out that understanding if you were in this position, as a leader at IGF.

Think about what information is relevant and not relevant in the media report—should anything be ignored? What other information about either player is relevant? Is there any consideration given to Tiger Woods' own much publicized moral conduct within his marriage? Is this relevant content or extraneous to this situation? Does this change anything about how you feel? What about the previous racist comments from Zoeller and Williams—are they relevant to this dilemma?

What do you think you would feel, see, or experience if you were in Tiger Woods' shoes at this point? What about if you were in Sergio Garcia's shoes?

OK, having got this far, the next thing to consider is your actual reaction to the story—how you think and feel about it personally?

For example, does the story include any "hot buttons" or likely "blind spots" for you? Is there anything or anyone that you personally feel very passionately about or that your own history and experiences are relevant to? An example could be if you or someone close to you have been involved in a racial vilification case, or you may have seen the devastation of lost sponsors and reputational damage in sport as a result of leadership inaction on sensitive social justice issues such as this before.

Which of your own biases come in to play here? Do you think that "casual banter" is a lame and over used excuse for poor behavior in sport or alternatively, that political correctness has gone too far and our communities are over sensitive and can't "have a laugh" anymore? Conversely, you might think that racism as a topic is just not taken seriously enough? Or maybe you think that sports people like Garcia are too often used for sociopolitical messaging. Do you have any biases or preconceptions about either player? What about the sport itself?

Which of your own virtues comes in to play here? These might include fairness, compassion, or courage, for example. If you hold these close to your heart, they will likely shape your view.

What do you think that sport should value most? This example gives us two main possibilities. On the one hand the protection, support, and sanctuary of an elite few who have dedicated their lives to being the best of the best and who role model performance excellence for the rest of us can be valued highly, and on the other hand, the opportunity to shape a social agenda on racial tolerance, using athletes and sports leaders as role-models for social inclusion might be valued highly. Both are completely relevant and reasonable, but on this occasion, they may seem to be in conflict at first glance. It is at this point that the ability to consider other perspectives, and understand where people are coming from becomes an essential tool.

Finally, on to the "D" in the ENDgame framework; judging your options and making a decision (Figure 5.4).

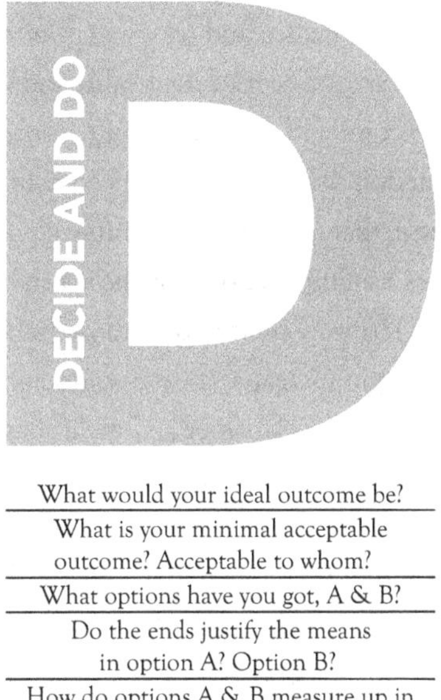

What would your ideal outcome be?

What is your minimal acceptable outcome? Acceptable to whom?

What options have you got, A & B?

Do the ends justify the means in option A? Option B?

How do options A & B measure up in terms of your stated organizational purpose, vision and values?

What will you choose?

What approach to voicing this decision will give you the most confidence and get an effective result?

Do you need to "rehearse" with a sounding board or ally?

In this decision and process is public knowledge tomorrow, does it sit well with you?

Figure 5.4 "D" of ENDgame framework

So what are you going to do—will you choose to sanction Garcia further or will you accept the apology as an adequate response to the incident?

One example analysis on this case might go something like this:

> The sports leaders frame the dilemma as whether to go easy on Sergio Garcia, who is willing to make amends in whatever way he can with Tiger Woods directly, and whom they believe is genuinely sorry for his remark (which they do see as racist even if the intent was not to harm), or whether to take the opportunity to demonstrate a strong and genuine commitment to getting rid of racism in the sport.

The leaders believe that racism and the perception of it that continues to dog the sport is too great a cost to the health and growth of golf, and certainly to players, current and future, whom racism may actually affect. They believe that inaction risks a view that they are only loosely committed to change, or worse, that they don't care and will protect their superstar assets at all costs. This has implications for the sports' reputation socially, commercially, and in terms of their appeal to corporate partners. At the same time, they see Sergio Garcia as a decent man who has contributed greatly to the sport both as a performer and an ambassador, and they are reluctant to allow him to become a media villain or make a scapegoat of him, particularly when other players over time are seen to have infringed in more severe ways and not demonstrated regret in the way Garcia has.

The leaders very much believe in the principles of equality and nondiscrimination, but they also want to be fair. They find themselves facing a value conflict between the desire to protect Garcia and the desire to respect an anti-discrimination agenda.

Primarily, the leaders see their duty as being to the health of the sport, with important but lesser duty owed to players, and then to the community at large.

There is concern among the leaders that if they allow "casual banter" to be used as an excuse for the harmful remark, they might implicitly sanction such behavior in future and provide a rationalization for racism (intentional or not). Their assumption is that Garcia is telling the truth about his intention, but it does not excuse the remark.

As far as Woods goes, the leaders feel that he has handled the situation elegantly and is, on the surface at least, unaffected by the incident as far as his on-going participation in the tournament. They are also assuming that Woods would prefer not to be at the center of major drama at this stage, but also that he would also be invested in progress on racism. It is agreed that these assumptions are to be tested in direct conversation with Woods. All other considerations about Tiger Woods' past are deemed completely irrelevant to the situation and this belief is spoken out loud within the group, particularly as one of the incumbent leaders presided over decisions regarding Woods' own future in the sport some years earlier in the face of his very public personal issues.

The leaders' wish to quickly address any anxiety and residual tension about the issue for both players involved, and they want to find a way to demonstrate both their compassion and courage in the face of this dilemma.

They believe that an ideal outcome would be that they take the opportunity to make progress on racism and position the sport well without this requiring Garcia's public humiliation.

The two options the leaders consider are as follows:

Option A: Take no further action involving Garcia, but embark on a significant program to address both social inclusion and racial discrimination within the game of golf at large. In addition, ensure that Woods is adequately supported further to the incident. This option risks public criticism and media scrutiny but is justified by the desire not to make a villain out of Garcia.

Option B: Request Garcia to engage in high-impact, private "awareness raising" conversations with subject matter experts to assist him to explore the problem of racism and casual banter more globally and beyond the incident at hand. Invite him subsequently to get involved in designing and/or delivering public awareness campaign on the values of social inclusion in sport as an alternative to personal sanctions such as suspensions or fines. In addition, ensure that Woods is adequately supported further to the incident. This option requires a potentially enforced early commitment from Garcia to the education; however, the leaders justify this in terms of making an investment in progress that will be both valuable for the individual, the sport, and the community in time.

The leaders decide to pursue option B, as it is deemed to best meet the desired outcomes and organizational vision without compromise: directly addresses Garcia's infringement and keeps the agenda authentic around progress rather than damage control.

The last question in the "D" column of the ENDgame framework, "if this process and outcome is public knowledge tomorrow, does it sit well with you?" is known as a *sunlight test*—basically a final check on how you would feel if your choice and your considerations were made known or "brought out into the sunlight" for all to see. In sport this may be in the form of a front-page headline, but also consider how you would feel if your family, friends, colleagues, boss, and those affected by the decision knew how, and why, you reached your judgment. Are you proud of it? Is there anything you are unsure of still?

Ethical decision making often involves conflicts of interest and values conflicts. Part of being an ethical leader is being prepared to sit with the discomfort of being unsure. You actually may not even like the decision (or certain consequences of the decision) but feel that it is the right one to make in the circumstances. You may feel that you would have liked to do more (for Woods, for Garcia, for golf, for the stakeholders etc.) but a different decision would not have added up ethically.

Once a decision has been made in this way, the tipping point for success is your commitment. The fact that you have worked out what the best option and the right thing to do is on balance of all considerations, does not make the doing carefree or easy. The deepest integrity is in your follow through as a leader.

Check-Out

It is one thing to use the ENDgame framework with a situation that does not involve you personally, as an exercise or rehearsal, but I also encourage you to take an example from your professional or personal life today, large or small, but meaningful for you and a genuine dilemma with ethical content, and try it out.

If you can't find a current example to use, try the framework with a past situation and see what your choice would be again today. It doesn't matter whether it is about sport leadership or not, it matters that your example is significant to you.

Whether you decided that an apology from Garcia to Woods was enough or not, you have used reason, logic, emotion, and a sense of what matters to you in your own character as a leader in your choice. You have considered numerous angles, and you have framed the ethical dilemma in a way that lets you respond in the best and fairest manner possible without being distracted by a range of inevitable pressures.

- It is useful to refer back to a framework to order your thinking and keep you on track. The ENDgame framework looks at the ethical content of an issue, the things you need to recognize about you and your processing, and the steps to judgment and making a decision. All that is left to do is to action that decision!
- There is not always an ideal answer or conclusion that you are completely comfortable with, but if you draw on reason and logic, on emotion and self-knowledge, and also on the characteristics that describe the person you strive to be, you are likely to be clearer and more considered than if you work off your gut alone. Ethical decision making doesn't have to involve absolutes.
- It is important to get clear about the actual dilemma that you need to work on—there is likely to be a lot of other important information you could consider, but it's not specific to what you need to decide on right now (like for example whether it is golf's job to work toward improved social attitudes on racism in the community *per se* rather than what you ought do about Garcia and the apology, or whether athletes should be role models for social attitudes or not).
- Wherever you are unsure, talk to a trusted ally, and share your reckoning and decision-making process. This is invaluable in terms of both clarity of and commitment to the outcome you reach.
- Making an ethical decision does not give any guarantee that the execution of that decision will be easier or more palatable for you. What it does do is let you rely on the fact that you have invested well in making the best available choice in the circumstances.

Our next chapter looks at some of the ways you can bring your decision to bear and voice your choices and your values when you have decided on what you ought to do.

CHAPTER 6

Making It Stick

Check-In

You have many choices about how to bring ethics to life in your organization, in terms of voicing your values, communicating your decisions, and shaping the culture and behavior that you wish to see. The greatest information about how best to "say it out loud" comes from your own life experiences and knowledge about what works best *for you*. As with ethical decision making, there are no absolutes or right ways, rather there are things that suit you and the circumstances best, and it is worth working out what they are if you are going to succeed.

This chapter helps you think about bringing your ethical practice to life from both the micro, individual level when you need to voice your position and your values on something now or in the short term, and also from the macro, organizational level in terms of what an organization can do over the longer term to normalize and integrate ethics in to everyday culture and practice.

This is about taking action, the penultimate piece in the puzzle.

Why Does This Matter?

Having to voice your values, including decisions you have made is a completely normal and inevitable part of life (let alone leadership), but it can require deft handling. If you have gone to the trouble of developing your ethical intelligence and invested in working through the ENDgame framework in order to make the best call on an issue at hand, there is no upside in either saying it out loud with unskilled or unplanned communication, or struggling to get it out at all.

Even on those occasions where you immediately know how you feel and where you stand on an issue and you don't need to do much "working through" at all, it can still be tricky to actually voice it out loud. Saying what you would like to say out loud can be hard for all sorts of reasons, including fear of retribution, fear of feeling isolated, and ostracized if others don't agree or dismiss what you have to say, anxiety about how others will see you—maybe as taking the moral high ground, thinking you are something special—or simply just not knowing how to say what you mean in a way that captures everything you feel.

All of these concerns add up to a lack of confidence, an essential resource. Without confidence, situations have the potential to feel out of control and threatening and we may be inclined to retreat, avoid, or procrastinate, or alternatively to aggress and put up defenses. The good news is of course that it is entirely possible to build both confidence and competence in saying it out loud.

Confidence in your ability to do something is built from positive experiences of success. Hence the importance of reflecting on what you want to achieve and what has worked and does work well *for you* in pursuit of those goals; that is what we will do here.

Discussion

The suggestions in this section are designed to help you to work out how to "make ethics stick" in your practice as a leader. At the individual level, this is about working out how you can say what you want to say out loud in a confident and competent manner. The best place to start is with your preferred style of communication.

What's Your Communication Style?

Each of us has a self-image that includes perceptions of what we are good at and not so good at. Knowing your preferred style allows you to play to your existing strengths.

Feedback is usually a good indicator of what you are good at. Ask yourself what is it that others have consistently recognized in you over time, as a strength? Are you best when you are communicating verbally or in written form? Are you more comfortable one on one, or in small or large groups? Are you known for being direct and certain in a way that allows everyone to know exactly where they stand? Or are you a "quiet achiever" influencing outcomes in more subtle and understated ways? What is it that works for you when you want to get an outcome? What do you do when you do *your best work*?

Equally important is working out the "no-go zones," or things that are most likely to make you uncomfortable, overwhelmed, or resistant. For some people this can represent having to tackle an intimidating authority figure, for others it is about the medium for conversation: in person, face-to-face, telephone, or written communication.

And then there is the prospect of the style of the person with whom you need to speak. If you anticipate that they will blow up like a pufferfish at any question of conduct, character, or values, leaving you in conflict and not in conversation, you may want to choose to raise the issue in a way that lets their angry or aggressive response deflate for a while before you can continue, such as an email or note. Equally, if you anticipate a recalcitrant response and a refusal to explore your concerns or position, you may choose to ensure you raise the issue when you have lots of time to persist, build trust, and help the person open up. Conversely, if you are communicating with someone who you anticipate will take the "retreat and avoid" position, you may want to be more direct. And in those circumstances where you cannot get a hearing at all and you feel you are being blocked, you may need to revisit the channels you are using to get your message across and recruit others to assist who may have more sway for various reasons, including formal authority or personal influence.

You have a choice about how you say it out loud every time you do so. The greater your understanding of what enables or disables you from communicating confidently, the more likely you are to have a successful outcome when you do communicate.

However, even seasoned leaders can struggle with voicing their values in different circumstances. Some situations just have more *bite;* they may feel more personal, more intimidating, or they may play to your own intentional and unintentional biases.

I have many examples, through my own career as a consulting psychologist in elite sport, that illustrate success and failure at saying it out loud in equal measure. Several times I have worried that speaking up would leave me as a pariah, on the outside and feeling awkward. This has particularly been the case if the topic at hand has been around comments that are sexist, as I am usually outnumbered as a woman in my professional sports environments and have sometimes found myself reluctant to draw further attention to differences. There are times where I have been stopped by stadium security on the way back to the locker room at full-time and told "it was no place for a woman." There are times when I have sat in executive and board meetings where sexist and crude commentary between men about an attractive female member of staff has been excused with "sorry love, just joking"; and times when I have pretended to be as amused as the men around me at a lewd, sexist joke in a work-social setting so that I could slide under the radar and escape uncomfortable and isolating attention; and times when teams have actually asked whether I plan to take time out for family reasons or whether they can rely on my commitment. But I have not been able to authentically say that the sexism *didn't* matter if I hadn't found a way to voice my values.

What has allowed me to progress, on this topic and others, has been developing an understanding of what action or approach I would be more likely to cope with. This usually starts with asking in my mind "what can I do here?" rather than "what if I don't act?"

For example, there was no way I was prepared to stand up and express my discomfort about the lewd joke while immersed in the social setting. I could predict that it would draw the very attention I did not want, "kill the mood", and result in people either rolling their eyes and turning away or feeling uneasy. That makes for hard work next time I am in a similar position. So I decided to "file it," knowing I would be spending ample time with these men across different settings, including intimate educational conversations about values and leadership, and I actually raised it months later as an example of a challenging value-based situation for me. The result was great; they understood and took more care.

However, the security guy, I felt, I could address there and then, and I chose to manage the situation with light-hearted humor. I smiled openly at him and made eye contact, telling him to look out because women were taking over. I took a moment to run through the various women involved in the team and what their (skilled and valuable) roles were, how long they'd been invested, and something they liked about the job. I asked him about his role, what he thought of the game, and we discussed my role and a little bit about what that involved, with which he became really engaged; I made it a conversation, between two people doing their job, and nothing to do with gender. Five or ten minutes in I said that I supposed a lot had changed over his time in the job, and it must be kind of different to see women so involved now. He agreed and spent a moment telling me what the old days were like, good and bad. I told him how much I valued working in sport and that I shared his love of the game. He wished me good luck for the following week.

Knowing your style, when it comes to voicing your values, takes time and personal reflection.

The following points might help you to find your own way to say it out loud.

When You Need to Voice Your Values

Prepare for the exchange:

- First get really clear on your viewpoint. Tell someone you trust what is on your mind and what you wish to convey or alternatively, write down **what** the issue is and what you think/feel about it that you wish to convey. It might be helpful to break it down in to 2 to 3 points if possible.
- Be clear about **why** you are raising this—what do you want to get out of the exchange? Is it the start of a longer discussion or a request for action, for example? Be prepared to respond if someone asks, "so what do you expect me to do about it?"
- Start from a position of respect for both the other person and their opinion, which may well be in opposition to yours. You may thoroughly disagree with an act, or dislike a position intensely whilst steering a respectful course toward voicing your position. It does not have to disintegrate into a personal battle if respect stays paramount.
- Accept that the person whom you are saying it out loud to may choose not to accept or act on what you raise. Think about what this will mean for you and what your next steps

might be before you first engage in the exchange. With the exception of those times where someone is obliged to do as you request, such as if you are charged with leveling a sanction for misconduct, you may have more work to do than you can achieve in one exchange. Alternatively, it may be that saying it out loud was actually enough for you in some cases and you don't feel the need to take it further.

- Work out **who** you should be talking to, who is the right audience for this conversation and if there is more than one person, should you address them in any particular order, or perhaps as a group?
- Many people find that they are able to lower stress by going off-line and having more intimate conversations one-on-one to start with. This will depend on "your way," however.
- It is valuable to enlist allies and sounding boards to check your thinking and give you feedback on whether what you want to say makes sense, sounds confident, and represents what you actually mean. A trusted source can offer you a *feeling response* too—how did they feel when they received what you said? Were they invited into a dialogue or told "how it is?" Did they feel that you were clear and that your ethical position was strong and non-negotiable but reasoned and fair? Did they feel that your concerns were focused on the issue and not the person? It may be that the right trusted source for you is not a work colleague, but a friend, family member, or coach outside of your organization.

During the exchange:

- Start with questions rather than assertions. In his book *The 7 Habits of Highly Effective People*, Stephen R. Covey lists habit five as "seek first to understand and then to be understood."[1] When you do this, you can listen well, during which time you get the opportunity to check out others' motivations, fears, and needs in regard to the situation. You also get clear about the whole story and have an opportunity to test any assumptions you are making. In addition, you buy yourself some time to orient yourself well and get comfortable in the conversation.

- Work through what you'd like to say step-by-step and try not to be rushed or sidetracked before you actually say what you mean. Obviously this doesn't have to be mechanical and forced, but confident and clear certainly helps. Think about the conditions and style that helps you to be confident and clear.
- When you raise a concern, it is useful to try and approach it from the perspective of helping someone to navigate the problem and the various choices in response to it, rather than simply telling them what they are doing wrong or what you don't like. Giving context and explaining why you want to talk about it assists this approach. It is also useful to appeal to shared alignment, shared values or purpose where you can within an exchange.
- When you can see assumptions, excuses, or the kind of "traps" we talk about in chapter 4, challenge them. Ask about them and open the discussion further.
- Compassion and empathy are great companions in the process of voicing your values and concerns, but they are only to be recruited if they are genuine. Patronization is likely to lose an open-ear. Be clear, definite, and respectful about your position.

For a really comprehensive insight and guide into voicing your values, see Mary Gentile's work on *Giving Voice to Values*.[2]

When You Want to Make Ethics Stick in Organizations

Outside of building your skills and confidence as an individual, there are myriad things you can do as a leader within your organization to embed the practice of ethics. Making it *stick* is not just about responding to things that go wrong, it is also about planning for what you would like to go right.

Here is some food for thought on normalizing ethical practice in your organization:

- One of the most important things you can do as a leader is to develop a consistent and visible *track record* of ethical leadership to show that you are *walking your talk*. This means getting in the habit and practice of taking care of issues and problems in a timely way, correcting wrongs, and seeking explanations and solutions rather than avoiding the hard stuff, and especially the hard *small* stuff. This embeds a culture of "doing" and a standard of behavior that is predictable to people. Your example is important, but don't presume that everybody gets to see what you and others do around ethics. It is important to deliberately and regularly tell the organizational stories of dealing with ethics, good and bad.
- As a leader, you can seek to ensure organizational value is placed on open debate and discussion. This needs to happen when things are going well not just when something is amiss. Lots of sports organizations have really robust mechanisms for managing issues, but what about the forums, meetings, and investment of time in planning for integrity (beyond compliance)—a lack of which can be a significant business risk.
- Consider the systems that your organization has in place for raising questions. Does this happen through personal alliances and informal channels, or do you also have room for neutral and confidential integrity officers to help people with ethical issues?
- Earlier we spoke about the risk of a "compliance" culture. The big issue with compliance only is that people can become focused on the fear of being caught doing something wrong, rather than on getting competent (and proud) of doing things right. Changing the narrative on ethics to be positive and aspiring, rather than negative and risk focused will aid buy-in.
- The documents, policies, systems, processes, and standards that underpin "your way" need to be explicit, congruent,

known, and accessible. Organizations can thrive when they have both leadership and mechanisms for success.

- Ethical standards within your organization should be non-negotiable and nondiscretionary. They only work if people can trust and believe in them and that requires fair and consistent application.
- Consider and discuss the organizational wider purpose when you invest in culture and ethics. What do you want the organizations legacy to be, and for whom? What is it that you want to be known for? How do you share this with other people in your organization?
- Develop a clear ethical framework or charter for your organization. This is different from a framework like the ENDgame decision-making framework, which is used to help you make an ethical choice. An ethical framework is more of a holistic charter that describes the organizations "way" including mission, vision, principles, beliefs, and values. Once developed, an ethical framework can be both an anchor and a rudder for a sound ethical culture.

Check-Out

You have a choice to act, and many times, you have a choice in how to act when it comes to bringing ethics to life as a leader. There is not a one-size-fits-all solution for voicing your values as an individual and different options are best at different times. You may choose to wait and act later, file the issue mentally and return to it at another time. You may choose to ask someone else for help. You don't have to have the courage of David in the face of Goliath in order to make a difference; being pragmatic is often a much better idea!

The values-driven behavior of sports leaders can be enormously impactful, and there is an incredible opportunity presented to sports people who are in the public eye in some way, either at the elite level or the community level, to model what they care about. It may be on a grand scale such as the UCI or IGF examples I have used in this book, or it may be on the pool deck of a school swimming carnival. Each is worthy of your intelligence and effort.

- Making ethics stick is partly about developing your confidence to voice your values on normal, everyday issues that you know need addressing in ways that are suited to you, and to the situation. There is no single right way to say what you need to say; it's better to work out your own style.
- One of the best indicators of what will work for you in future is what has worked for you before. Reflect on it, and ask others for feedback on your communication strengths.
- Where possible, take time to prepare in order to have a successful exchange when you want to voice your values. There are many times where it is possible to step back and plan how you want to tackle something rather than just jump straight in.
- A sensible start point for developing organizational ethics is to develop an ethical framework or charter in consultation with your team. This process facilitates meaningful conversations about what matters to the organization and solidifies a position that you can communicate and utilize day to day.

CHAPTER 7

Your Role As an Ethical Leader

Check–In

The final piece of the puzzle is you as the leader. What does this all mean for you personally? Not just in terms of your leadership practice, but beyond that to your beliefs, attitudes, and expectations of yourself and of others? You will have got the message by now that the whole topic of ethical leadership is *personal.* This is where it differs from other forms of competency to some degree. Optimally, ethics is not something we do separately from who we believe we are.

Knowing your own heart, mind, and spirit is a critical starting point. Self-awareness, including awareness of those explicit biases that you have and the likely blind spots in your rational and emotional processing of information, is a great advantage in ethics. We can think and feel our way through ethics, and it is often deeply connected to whom we believe we are (our characters). Where any of us can find a potent reason for a decision, what Jeffrey Kotter refers to as "a truth that influences what we *feel,*" we are more likely to find the motivation to follow the decision through to action.[1]

In the following pages I explore several concepts around leadership that can help you consider *you,* within your role as an ethical leader in sport. Each of these offers a vantage point from which to observe your own performance, strengths, limitations, and biases.

Discussion

It seems to me that effective leaders in sport do several things consistently, and that the most rewarding and authentic experience of leadership is arguably underpinned by a couple of strong philosophies.

Behaviors

The first thing that effective leaders do is that they **make it clear who is in charge** with nothing left to assumption. This does not equate to rampant autocrats who impose themselves upon others. It means that good leaders acquire and exercise different types of power effectively. Social psychologists John R. P. French and Bertram Raven noted five bases of power: legitimate, reward, coercive, expert, and referent.[2] Effective leaders are in charge not just because their job title and corner office decrees it so, or because the consequences of not bowing to their power are too grave, but also because they are *technically competent* or expert as leaders, which means they can be trusted and relied upon. People within and outside the organization are clear on who is leading because the effective leader has also acquired *referent power,* which means that others have a high level of identification with, admiration of, or respect for the leader. Effective leaders understand the relationship between power and influence.

Second, effective leaders **work on their own leadership attributes** once they are in the role of leader, not just when they are rehearsing and training for it. These attributes include the competencies of an ethical leader (examples of competencies are outlined in the appendix to this book) and speak strongly to credibility, to interpersonal skills, particularly empathy, and to the developing of emotional intelligence, which frames in part the way you understand what is happening around you.

Third, effective leaders **make the tough calls**. They fix what is broken quickly and decisively without resorting to being rash or crude in their actions. The time it takes to actually understand the context and detail of a situation may vary significantly, case to case; effectiveness is not about speed alone. Effective leaders refer to their thoughts, reason, *and* their feelings about difficult decisions, not presuming one to be superior to the others. There has been no solid evidence to suggest that intuition or "gut feel" is not important and valid information in decision making, and much good support for the case that what we learn in the first couple of seconds of rapid cognition when we engage with a situation or person, is critical.[3] Effective leaders draw on each of these sources of data to work out what to do, but once things are clear, they don't hedge, they act and they accept the cost.

Fourth, effective leaders **empower other people so that they can collaborate in the building of a high-performance organization.** Empowerment isn't just about saying "yes" or asking people to use their initiative and exercise their own creativity on tasks. It involves spending time and resource on letting people know and understand the "why" as well as the "what" you hope to achieve, and exploring objectives that actually align with the why and what at all levels of the organization. It takes depth of conversation to build alliances and trust enough that you can let go, and others can take the reins. It seems that under ever increasing pressure for bigger returns, organizations can confuse "get it off my desk and on to someone else's" with "empowerment." In sport, one thing that I have observed in successful teams is that once athletes are empowered, for example, as a captain, or as a leadership group, they must be genuinely able to make decisions alongside management in pressure situations, especially if those situations involve a team mate. It is damaging to athlete trust, confidence, and buy-in if a leadership group is told that they have authority, but it is taken away from them if their decision or input is inconvenient or difficult to manage. True empowerment encourages diverse input.

Empowerment also involves giving people the resources and competencies they need to achieve the objectives you set. It is disempowering and shortsighted to sell a vision that is beyond reach and ask people just to stretch further. There are many examples through sport, business, and indeed, life of people achieving extraordinary things with seemingly inadequate resources, but as a regular expectation this can quickly become fatiguing and manipulative. Self-starters and go-getters run out of steam too.

Finally, to empower people it is important to let them know honestly the rules of the game, what boundaries they can work in, and examples of situations that you envisage they would need to escalate or get permission for, from you or others. Empowerment isn't the same as *cut-loose* to do as one pleases, nor is being empowered in any way being unaccountable. The leader needs to ask for regular updates and give regular feedback alongside an empowered team.

Fifth, effective leaders **don't allow people to get too cozy with the status quo**. In fact, they make sure people are dissatisfied with the status quo and they breed a culture that expects change and is successful at implementing it. This is not the same as breeding a culture of fear, where people anxiously look over their shoulder and feel restricted in their views or endeavors. It is simply about creating an expectation of regular progress and high standards, where the questions what else? or what next? are welcomed. Effective leaders continually enunciate what the organizational objectives and expectations are; they continually sell the vision and the plan for change.

If there is immovable resistance to change or a dysfunctional and negative culture, an effective leader will change the senior leadership first before seeking to change, teach, or remove anyone else. Modeling at the top of an organization is critical. It is very difficult to get buy-in to progress elsewhere in an organization if people don't feel that those at the top of the tree walk their talk. Sometimes this is about avoidance of initiatives rather than overt verbal resistance. This is the same within teams; if there is one athlete, maybe a superstar performer who sits outside the rules, or refuses to change, and is not addressed, there is a high risk of cynicism, disquiet, and resistance among the rest of the team. An example of this is the athlete who refuses to adapt to new advances in medical recovery practices or physical preparation routines, or who consistently skips compulsory meetings or workshops without recourse for not fulfilling their obligations to the team.

Finally, effective leaders in sport know how to **exploit the language of leadership**. Great coaches have always known how to do this and get the most out of people, inspire and rouse commitment, but you may think that what you do day in and day out needs to be different to what a coach does mid-performance. Not always. The common ground is in speaking to what will connect with your audience *first*. Skilled communication is consistent, clear, and reaches the right people. But there is science to effective leadership language. An effective leader is a storyteller who understands that humans respond to emotion and symbols that offer meaning and context before they get to reason.[4] Effective leaders think about *how* they say things in order to optimize their influence, not just the details and data in what they say. For leaders with high levels of charisma, this comes easily, but for any effective leader, it is a necessary skill. When the emotion you communicate is authentic and true for you, it is likely to be most powerful, not least on questions of ethics and integrity.

Concepts

Underpinning our overt behaviors (or at least those that we are conscious of) is a set of beliefs. We examined this in the Lance Armstrong case study in chapter 3; how different a decision or action might be depending on your core beliefs and the principles you work from. Leadership is no different; what you believe will steer your behavioral course.

Possibly one of the strongest and most useful concepts around leadership in sport that I have encountered debunks the belief that leaders should be perfect and infallible. This is the **Good Enough Leader** concept.

Good enough leadership is about developing an authentic leadership practice that doesn't rely on the myth of being perfect. Far from resting with mediocre, "good enough" encourages resilience in the face of challenges by embracing all the normal and obvious realities of being flawed and human while we lead.

The concept was developed by British Jungian psychoanalyst, Andrew Samuels in his book *The Good Enough Leader.*[5] Samuels based his work on Donald Winnicott's concept of "the good enough mother" (and later adaptations of "the good enough parent").[6] Winnicott described the role of the mother as being able to *fail the child at a rate that it can tolerate,* so that it might develop and become self-sufficient, learning about the mother's limitations in a constructive way. The role of mother is still vital, just not omnipotent. Samuels applies this to leadership by pointing out the vital role of failure. A good enough leader is an "artist in failure" and can do so constructively without the sting, blame, or scorn and with an understanding of the normality and utility of stuffing things up now and then. This is a central part of resilience and potentially where resilience differs from the old-fashioned notions of hardness or toughness that suggest uncompromising, rigid, unmovable, rather than durable, strong, and able to shift or grow.

Samuels also proposes that there is a psychological gap between our heads and hearts when it comes to thinking about leadership. Intellectually, most of us realize that the stereotypically masculine, gung-ho, war-like leaders are no good for us on the whole, but we continue to have a love affair with the heroic leader. They excite us. But the status of hero cannot accommodate failure. It is an idealized fantasy of leadership where the illusion of being in-charge must prevail at all costs and there is scarcely room for doing your best, not seeing something coming, or being unprepared. When the inevitable ambiguity, uncertainty, messiness, error, confusion, or anxiety pop up for leaders, and they don't know what to do or they fail, they are denigrated and often treated harshly. The end result of course is fear and a culture of perfectionism and obsessive striving. Nobody wants to put a foot wrong, and they may not choose to tell you if they do. Perhaps there is a place for sincere apologies and graceful acceptance of them in good enough leadership, where people are accepted as imperfect.

I observed an excellent example of the power of being willing to show vulnerability around failure sometime back from a leader in a sporting organization I was working with. In the face of a very public off-field scandal for the organization, he had overridden a decision on a marketing campaign that a senior executive had spent several months developing and brought in a PR specialist from another field to rewrite the communications messaging over a period of about a week. He had basically panicked, and felt a sense of urgency and pressure to control some of the damage caused by the scandal. The PR campaign certainly addressed the relevant messaging in relation to the scandal, but missed many other markers and was in effect a failure on the whole. It left the executive feeling undervalued and disempowered and the rest of the organization confused. After some reflection, the leader called his executives together, saying he needed to discuss something with them about the recent marketing campaign. He started the conversation with "I stuffed that right up didn't I? I didn't listen and I panicked a bit under pressure. The campaign was a failure. Can I ask you to help me think about what we can do next to address this, guys?" Much honest conversation ensued, and the response was overwhelmingly positive because he accepted his mistake and the failure openly. This quickly translated to respect and a drive to support him.

Perfectionism is a quick highway to exhaustion and disempowerment, where people are discouraged from taking personal responsibility. The alternative is to embrace all of our "untidy" humanness and work toward wholeness, not perfection. To do so is liberating. To see the parameters of what is achievable, plausible, and realistic allows you to innovate within those parameters, to choose wisely where to expend your energy. Perfection is a myth and once you shake that construct off, the possibility for growth and achievement is improved no matter where you start and no matter your view of human nature.

Good enough isn't about being average. It's about sustainable and redefined success.

In a brilliant essay first delivered at the United States Military Academy at West Point and published in the *American Scholar* in 2010, William Deresiewicz introduces a second important concept, that of **solitude in leadership.**[7]

Deresiewicz argues that one of the most important necessities of true leadership is solitude, because it is only in solitude that we can truly reflect on what we each believe in, what we care about, and how it is evolving over time, and it is only in solitude that we can learn to actually think things through for ourselves rather than buy someone else's wisdom wholesale.

The premise that Deresiewicz starts from is that there is a dearth of true thinkers because what is rewarded above all else in most contemporary organizations is conformity: leaders who know how to "keep the routine going"—a routine of growth, profit, or winning *because that's what we do* and leaders who know who to be, who to be with, and which ladder to climb to get ahead. He describes a leadership community that is composed of people who can answer questions but don't know how to ask them and who can think about how to get things done but not whether they are worth doing in the first place. He talks about people who become excellent at one specific thing and have no interest in anything beyond their own area of expertise. Deresiewicz's call to action is a call for people with independent minds, who will buck the system *if and when* it needs bucking (but not for the sake of it), who feel free and confident to express disagreement, and who see it as their responsibility not to tolerate the unethical.

An example of being willing to take a solo path and think independently in sports leadership was given by the Australian Football League (AFL) in 2005. Despite significant pressure from the various forces of government across Australian sport and anti-doping, and eventually world anti-doping, the league and the AFL Players' Association collectively decided to stand apart and develop a drug policy that they felt at the time better reflected and addressed the issue at hand within their sport. Far from being maverick in design, their approach was based on the counsel of medical experts and world best practice on harm minimization around drug use, but it stood independent to all other Australian sports at the time. This meant that while the league abided by the WADA policy on performance-enhancing drugs, it separately introduced a three-strike policy on illicit drug use, designed with the dual purpose of offering deterrents to care for athletes who may have drug problems. It would only be after three strikes for drug use that an athlete would face suspension from the game. Earlier infringements would result in a regime of education and treatment for the athlete managed by the AFL Medical Association independent of clubs and in fact the league or Players' Association. This did not comply with the government's preferred sanction-based two-strike policy, and the AFL's policy came under very heavy fire for being soft on drugs. Nevertheless, the CEOs and boards of both the AFL and the AFL Players Association were willing to stand their ground because they had thought independently about what they believed mattered most. They had asked different and confronting questions of their own sport, explored in collaboration, but been prepared to make judgments in solitude.

It requires courage to argue your ideas when they are not popular, but a different kind of courage than the heart-stopping physical bravery and public exposure that we are used to seeing in spades in sport, and that is moral courage. Again this raises the question of the cost, because the courage it takes to stop, resist, challenge, and say "no" can get in the way of heavily embedded values like loyalty or unity within sports organizations and teams. It is only when you really know who you are and what matters to you, understanding formed in solitude, that you will step away from the crowd and accept the cost of being an independent thinker.

Solitude in leadership doesn't necessarily mean being alone though. In fact, Deresiewicz suggests that the time spent in intimate conversation with a trusted friend is where you might get to know yourself best, so long as you feel safe enough to ask the questions you are supposed to know the answer to, and to raise the doubts you are not supposed to have. Whatever your friend replies, the investigation of your own mind is prized.

The third important leadership concept is about **trust.** In essence, most of the discussion in this book intersects with trust in some way: trust in yourself, and what matters to you, trust in a framework to enable your ethical decision making, and trust enough to voice your values when you know what's right or wrong. This leadership approach also emphasizes being able to demonstrate your own trustworthiness and your ability to place trust in others. The bottom line is how important do you believe it is to do what you say you are going to do?

Real trust happens between people when you move beyond a "calculus" model, where one person extends trust *because of what they expect in return* (which may include loyalty, favoritism, in-group belonging, or rewards for example), to a relationship in which trust is extended and expected automatically as a normal, demonstrable, quantifiable part of engagement between people. Trust is built when we see and feel people acting with integrity and when we see them competently and consistently delivering on what they say they are going to do. In his book, *The Speed of Trust*, Stephen M. R. Covey describes how readily and instantly trust can be created (or destroyed) between people, and the extraordinary significance of trust as a performance factor to be leveraged in organizational leadership.[8] This lays to rest the belief that trust is hard earned and permanent, illuminating instead the fact, that every leader needs to invest regularly in trust as an underpinning approach.

Those sports' leaders who adopt specific trust building practices with their colleagues, their team, their members, fans, their stakeholders and partners are able to appeal to the values other people hold and offer the opportunity for alignment. In effect, this means you immediately begin proving your competence, character, and credibility and people are likely to be more open to you, in good times and bad. The old school top-down leadership model in sport of reverting to command-and-control leadership when something goes wrong is defeating when it comes to trust. Controlling what people know and how they interact only creates a climate of fear and absolves people of responsibility. Battening down the hatches leaves you inside and everyone else outside. Even when things have gone horribly wrong, if people know what you are doing and why, you can still appeal to their values. Transparent and clear communication is fundamental to building trust, engagement, and commitment, and it starts at the top.

My intention in presenting you with these three concepts is to encourage you to think about your own character, credibility, and competence as a leader, because you are the instrument of your work when you are leading. The results you achieve are *through* your leadership, but the art of leadership itself, is *within* you.

On the topic of your role as an ethical leader, it would be remiss of me not to talk about the importance of you coaching other people on ethics. Leadership has a strong teaching and guiding element and supporting people to find meaning in things outside of targets, bottom line results, their own niches of expertise, and grinding through another onslaught of tabloid headlines can create a very different return on investment over time. And it does take time. An ethical framework should be something cultivated collectively and not imposed from on-high; you can't tell people what their own meaning should be. A part of your job as an ethical leader is to patiently and pragmatically teach people how to make good decisions that manage risk while bringing values to life. It is also about having *different conversations* about what it means to win, to gain competitive advantage, and to be successful. It is especially important to recognize that people under pressure are more likely to consider shortcuts and ethical compromises. What is it that you emphasize in your organization, and at what cost?

A sound indicator of how healthy your leadership is in this vein is to observe how people talk about values and ethics in your organization and who they talk about when they do. If you hear a single person, especially yourself, being referred to as the moral compass or the straight arrow (what Jill Geisler has referred to as "the sole ethics guru") in the business, you might want to check how confident and ready people feel to voice their values and do ethics themselves and not pass the buck.[9]

Check-Out

In summary, I want to reiterate that there are probably so many more times you have got ethical leadership right than times that you have got it wrong. Take the time to evaluate your success and not just your mistakes or gaps. The beauty about ethical leadership being personal is that you have a lifetime of experience to draw on. Now you also have the END-game framework to help you work through decisions and dilemmas, and hopefully a clearer or more ordered understanding of how to approach ethical leadership in sport.

- When we draw on our character and our own ethos, our ability to reason and use logic, and also the way we feel about things, we use broad and valid sources of data that can inform our progress.
- Good leaders act decisively to fix what they know is wrong. They face reality and don't shy away from the hard conversations. But power and influence in leadership do not have to rely on old-school command and control systems that close off discussion. Open, transparent communication is often much less risky in terms of trust.
- Good leaders invest time and resource in building the capacity of those around them to do well on ethics and avoid being seduced into the guru role.
- Three leadership concepts, accepting that good enough leaders are human and imperfect, being able to think things through for yourself and away from the pack in solitude, and assuming trust to be the non-negotiable foundation to good ethical leadership, offer a platform for sound practice.
- The balance of moral courage and pragmatism is critical in ethical leadership. There is nothing that necessitates being a sole crusader or a hero on ethics at the expense of organizational performance. Reliably delivering results remains a fundamental, but equal, priority.
- Ethics is not a perfect science and none of us will ever be perfect leaders, but winning in this context means playing to your strengths, deepening your integrity and "staying thinking." The endeavor of ethical leadership *in itself* allows us to thrive.

APPENDIX

Being Competent As an Ethical Leader

Getting competent at anything requires practice, yet we don't always have the time to "go back to the books" and revise what it is we are supposed to do when we face a challenge. Leaders often need "just-in-time" learning as they hit problems in the workplace that need fast attention and can't wait for scheduled learning time. For this reason, it is important to *notice* and learn from your experiences past and present and reflect on them and yourself as you go.

It can also help to map out where you want to get to (albeit not finite) and check in on your progress. Ethical practice is probably no more esoteric than many other aspects of leadership, so why not develop yourself on it in the same way you would with other leadership competencies?

Following are some examples of benchmark competencies in ethical leadership for you to reference yourself against; a measure of where you are at and what you will likely be doing when you are both competent and confident as an ethical leader.

Consider what it is that you want to be good at as an ethical leader? How would the leader that you *want* to be act? Where do you sit in relation to those ideals at the moment?

A leadership competency is basically the skills and behaviors (underpinned by knowledge) that are required to excel, or in philosophical terms, to flourish. Competencies can be built into career and coaching plans, performance reviews, or simply used as a personal guide.

The following benchmark competencies for *culture-focused leaders* were developed for a corporate client of mine in partnership with my colleague Naomi Harrison from Psych Insight in Australia.[1]

Each competency is divided to represent a developmental pathway, giving a description and examples of what you might expect to see in yourself (or others) early in your career, once you have been operating for some time—say 5 years plus (mid-career)—and once you take on leadership roles.

Competencies of Culture Leaders

Commitment and Intention

Definition: Recognizes and seeks opportunity to achieve and progress on a sound, high-performing culture. Overtly makes excellence and ethics equal priorities. Persists with high energy and intensity in the face of challenges. Stands up and uses voice on difficult issues.

Early career

1. Committed to high personal standards and continuous improvement.
2. Includes ethics in stated goals and objectives when planning processes and outcomes.
3. Acts and communicates in a way that supports the organizational culture and values.

Mid-career/individual contributor level

1. Committed to high personal standards and continuous improvement and encourages the same in others.
2. Commits own resources (especially time) to the development of a sound, high-performing culture.
3. Invests time in getting it right in tough times as well as good times and speaks up when things go awry or fall short of the mark.

Leader

1. Role models high standards and continuous improvement and fosters them in others.

2. Takes a leadership position on developing a sound, high-performing culture.
3. Represents, espouses, and teaches the organizational ethical framework, including when facing dilemmas or when values come into conflict.

Ethical Intelligence

Definition: Organizational and personal ethics inform behavior. Understands sound culture and high performance as unshakable partners in sustained achievement within the organization. Utilizes relevant tools, models, and resources in solving difficult ethical challenges or dilemmas.

Early career

1. Draws on ethical conscience to inform behavior. Asks "Does this feel right?" and "How can I improve things if not?"
2. Factors care, justice, respect, and responsibility into working methods.

Mid-career/individual contributor

1. Asks ethical questions such as "Where are we going?" "Who gains and who loses?" and "Is this development desirable?" in progress toward excellence.
2. Balances practicality and results drive with goodwill and positive character when pursuing goals.

Leader

1. Provides guidance on ethical questions in progress toward excellence.
2. Puts time and effort into guiding own and others ethical thinking and practice.

Cultural Literacy

Definition: Understands and displays the organizations ethical framework and desirable behaviors. Translates and communicates to others. Considers the cultural imprint and legacy of behaviors in intent and actions.

Early career

1. Knows the signature practices of the organization that support the organizational values and principles.
2. Displays organizational values and principles in work plans and everyday actions.

Mid-career/individual contributor

1. Knows and consistently displays the signature practices of the organization that supports the organizational values and principles.
2. Considers the imprint that own attitudes and behaviors leave on colleagues, customers (fans, members, sport consumers), and other stakeholders beyond today and displays strong and consistent distinguishing behaviors in line with organizational ethical framework.

Leader

1. Embodies and develops in others the signature practices of the organization that support the organizational values and principles.
2. Develops a strong cultural legacy through shared ideas, beliefs, and appropriate habits. Shares examples and stories of positive culture with team.

Develops Moral Character

Definition: Lives the values and principles of the organization. Recognizes and acts on personal, organizational, and social responsibilities, and considers the interests of the broader community. Demonstrates organizational and social citizenship.

Early career

1. Displays respect, trustworthiness, and honesty everyday.
2. Says and does what was committed to in relation to personal and community responsibilities.
3. Shows organizational citizenship behaviors such as loyalty and willingness to help colleagues.

Mid-career/individual contributor

1. Displays respect, trustworthiness, and honesty everyday.
2. Says and does was committed to in relation to personal and community responsibilities and expects the same of others.
3. Shows organizational citizenship behaviors such as loyalty and willingness to help colleagues.
4. Displays willingness to "do the right thing" by communities in which the organization operates.

Leader

1. Displays respect, trustworthiness, and honesty everyday, and reinforces in team.
2. Demonstrates commitment to personal, organizational, and wider social and community responsibilities.
3. Models organizational citizenship behaviors such as loyalty and willingness to help colleagues in order to achieve larger organizational objectives.
4. Shapes opportunities to "do the right thing" by communities in which the organization operates.

Open Communication

Definition: Is clear, concise, and open when communicating with all stakeholders. Listens to and acknowledges input of others. Adjusts communication to different audiences and is authentic in communications.

Early career

1. Speaks in a clear, concise manner.
2. Open to what others have to say. Listens, asks questions to increase clarity, checks own understanding, and does this consistently.
3. Speaks up about doubts or concerns; balances candor with diplomacy.

Mid-career/individual contributor

1. Communicates with clarity, efficiency, and honesty, using a variety of channels.
2. Seeks to understand different people and different communication styles. Listens, asks questions to increase clarity, checks understanding, and invites the views of others to challenge thinking. Does this consistently so that communication is always authentic.
3. Openly raises issues and responds to challenging questions confidently and constructively.

Leader

1. Communication is clear, succinct, and transparent in all mediums.
2. Tailors communication to values and goals of the organization and concerns of the person. Actively listens to understand different perspectives. Asks questions, checks understanding, and encourages others to express points of view even if difficult or contentious. Helps determine priorities to keep communication effective.
3. Holds an open agenda with direct and indirect stakeholders and ensures goals are clear and shared within and across teams. Does this consistently so that communication is always authentic.

Impact and Influence

Definition: Communicates clearly and persuasively to convince, influence, engage, or impress others, using appropriate mediums, and with respect.

Early career

1. Communicates in a clear and concise manner to ensure a positive impact.
2. Shows integrity in all interactions.
3. Takes time to listen to others and understand where they're coming from.

Mid-career/individual contributor

1. Communicates credibly and persuasively to ensure a positive impact.
2. Tailors communication to suit the audience and uses a range of influencing techniques to build support.
3. Shows integrity in all interactions.
4. Supports others and speaks positively about all parts of the business.

Leader

1. Generates interest and understanding of ideas through clear and persuasive communication.
2. Builds support by taking the time to educate and consult others.
3. Displays and encourages integrity in all interactions.

Self-Development

Definition: Actively reflects on own character, attitudes, and behaviors and proactively manages own learning. Seeks feedback from others to understand own strengths and areas of development, to improve own performance and live a balanced, purposeful, and healthy life.

Early career

1. Actively reflects on own attitudes, behaviors, and performance. Recognizes and can articulate areas of strength and development.
2. Is open to feedback from others.

3. Takes responsibility for own learning, including seeking and incorporating feedback from others to inform own development, and reflecting on and learning from mistakes.
4. Effectively balances work/life goals.

Mid-career/individual contributor

1. Actively reflects on own character, attitudes, and behavior.
2. Is open and actively seeks feedback from others through formal and informal channels.
3. Utilizes personal reflection and acquisition of new skills and knowledge to improve performance and learn from mistakes.
4. Seeks to live a balanced, purposeful life.

Leader

1. Creates a learning environment that continually seeks personal excellence; sets an example through own learning endeavors and reflections.
2. Keeps up to date technically and professionally.
3. Sees mistakes and setbacks as part of own and others' development.
4. Proactively seeks feedback from others.
5. Accepts feedback in a nondefensive and objective manner.
6. Seeks to live a balanced, purposeful life and supports others in their efforts for the same.

Judgment and Decision Making

Definition: Grasps information quickly, gathers all the relevant data but is not paralyzed or delayed by over thinking. Weighs out the pros and cons, costs and benefits to the organization. Cuts through ambiguous data and information to make decisions. Supports judgments and decisions with rationale, and makes just, practical, and culturally faithful decisions.

Early career

1. Breaks down a problem into simple list of tasks or activities. Sees essential similarities between current situation and things that have happened before.
2. Applies knowledge or methods taking into account business and ethical considerations.

Mid-career/individual contributor

1. Systematically breaks down problems into manageable parts to reach a solution. Thinks through "what if" scenarios to identify all the possible implications of a proposed course of action.
2. Gathers relevant data from a wide range of sources and eliminates unnecessary information. Makes connections between information.
3. Probes to understand root causes.
4. Ensures decision making is focused on the most relevant issues and makes culturally faithful, commercially considered, and ethical decisions.

Leader

1. Sees patterns and makes connections between information. Identifies patterns in qualitative and quantitative data.
2. Takes apart complex problems and situations and analyses from a number of different angles. Looks at cause and effect relationships.
3. Recommends a range of potential solutions after weighing all the pros and cons, including ethical and commercial considerations.
4. Thinks about issues, the consequences, timeliness, and cost of different decisions and longer term implications across the organization (or sport).
5. Facilitates thoughtful, robust, ethical thinking, and problem solving with others.
6. Conclusions are well thought through and considered. Understands the consequences of information.

Notes

Introduction

1. St. James Ethics Centre (2010).
2. Kotter and Heskett (1992).

Chapter 1

1. Ablow (2013).
2. Rice (1920); de Coubertin (1894).
3. Frontier Economics Report (2010).
4. Australian Bureau of Statistics: 4156 (2012).
5. Frontier Economic Report (2010).
6. Australian Bureau of Statistics: 4156 (2012).
7. Australian Bureau of Statistics: 6285 (2010).
8. Frontier Economics Report (2010)
9. ATKearney (2011)
10. Australian Bureau of Statistics: 4156.0.55.002 (2013)
11. Enoch (n.d.).
12. Australian Bureau of Statistics: 4174 (2009-10)
13. Aly (2012).
14. Flanagan (2011).
15. Carroll (2008).
16. Anderson (1991).

Chapter 2

1. Longstaff (2009).
2. Gentile (2010).
3. Kidder (2006).
4. Shockley-Zalabak (1999).
5. Messick and Tenbrunsel (2004).
6. Rest (1986).
7. Bazerman and Tenbrunsel (2011).
8. Bazerman and Tenbrunsel (2011).
9. Clarke (2013).
10. Vincent Fairfax Fellowship (Ethics in Leadership).

Chapter 3

1. Singer (1993).
2. Le Guin (1973).
3. Ross (1930).
4. The Associated Press (2012). Used with permission of The Associated Press Copyright© 2013. All rights reserved.

Chapter 4

1. Durant (n.d.).
2. ethicsalarm.com (n.d.).
3. Gandhi (1993).
4. Collins (2012).
5. Gilchrist (2008).

Chapter 5

1. The Independent Copyright © (2013): www.independent.co.uk

Chapter 6

1. Covey (2004).
2. Gentile (2010).

Chapter 7

1. Kotter and Cohen (2002).
2. French and Raven (1959).
3. Gladwell (2005).
4. Pinker (1994).
5. Samuels (2001).
6. Winnicott (1953).
7. Deresiewicz (2010).
8. Covey (2006).
9. Geisler (n.d.).

Appendix

1. Harrison; Grange (2012).

References

Ablow, K. (2013, April). *Sports don't matter, not one iota.* Retrieved on April 6, 2013, from Fox News: http://www.foxnews.com/opinion/2013/04/06/sports-dont-matter-not-one-iota/

Aly, W. (2012). *Gold is good.* Retrieved on September 2012, from The Monthly: http://www.themonthly.com.au/issue/2012/september/1347451633/waleed-aly/gold-good

Anderson, B. R. O'G. (1991). In *Imagined communities: Reflections on the origin and spread of nationalism* (Revised and extended ed.), p. 224. London, England: Verso.

ATKearney. *The sport market: Major trends and challenges in an industry full of passion*, 2011. Retrieved from: http://www.atkearney.com.au/documents/10192/6f46b880-f8d1-4909-9960-cc605bb1ff34

Australian Bureau of Statistics: 4156—*Sports and Physical Recreation: A Statistical Overview*, Australia, 2012. Retrieved from: http://www.abs.gov.au/ausstats/abs@.nsf/Latestproducts/4156.0Main%20Features12012?opendocument&tabname=Summary&prodno=4156.0&issue=2012&num=&view=

Australian Bureau of Statistics: 6285—*Involvement in organized Sport and Physical Activity*, Australia, 2010. Retrieved from: http://www.abs.gov.au/ausstats/abs@.nsf/Latestproducts/6285.0Main%20Features4April%202010?opendocument&tabname=Summary&prodno=6285.0&issue=April%202010&num=&view=

Australian Bureau of Statistics: 4156.0.55.002—*Value of Sport, Australia, 2013*. Retrieved at: http://www.abs.gov.au/AUSSTATS/abs@.nsf/Lookup/4156.0.55.002Chapter272013

Australian Bureau of Statistics: 4174—*Spectator Attendance at Sporting Events, 2009–10*. Retrieved from: http://www.abs.gov.au/ausstats/abs@.nsf/Products/4174.0~2009-10~Main+Features~Introduction?OpenDocument

Bazerman, M. H., & Tenbrunsel, A. E. (2011). *Blind spots: Why we fail to do what's right and what to do about it*. Princeton, NJ: Princeton University Press

Carroll, J. (2008). *Ego and soul: The modern west in search of meaning*. Melbourne, Australia: Scribe.

Clarke, L. (2013, April 7). Rutgers abuse case offers window into an imbalance of power. *The Washington Post*.

Collins, M. (2012). *Three years after Bloodgate, renaissance man O'shea has restored Quins' reputation.* Retrieved on September 29, 2012, from Mail Online: http://www.dailymail.co.uk/sport/rugbyunion/article-2210570/Conor-OShea-restored-reputation-Harlequins.html

Covey, S. M. R. (2006). *The SPEED of trust: The one thing that changes everything* (1st ed.). New York, NY: Free Press.

Covey, S. R. (2004). *The 7 habits of highly effective people: Powerful lessons in personal change*. New York, NY: Free Press.

de Coubertin, P. (1894). *It's not the winning it's the taking part.*

Deresiewicz, W. (2010). *Solitude and leadership.* Retrieved on 2010, from The American Scholar: http://theamericanscholar.org/solitude-and-leadership/#.UvndYPuOuhM

Durant, W. (n.d.). *Quotation details.* Retrieved from Quotations Page: http://www.quotationspage.com/quote/1370.html#note

Enoch, W. (n.d.). *Submission: Australian Publishers Association (APA).* Retrieved from Creative Australia: http://creativeaustralia.arts.gov.au/submission/australian-publishers-association-apa/

Unethical rationalizations and misconceptions (n.d.). Retrieved from Ethics Alarms: http://ethicsalarms.com/rule-book/unethical-rationalizations-and-misconceptions/

Flanagan, M. (2011). *Muslim and Jewish footballers proving they're all of a peace.* Retrieved on September 19, 2011, from The Age: http://www.theage.com.au/victoria/muslim-and-jewish-footballers-proving-theyre-all-of-a-peace-20110918-1kg2o.html

French, J. R. P., & Raven, B. (1959). The bases of social power. In D. Cartwright & A. Zander (eds.), *Group dynamics*. New York, NY: Harper & Row.

Frontier Economics Report. (2010). *The economic contribution of sport to Australia.* Retrieved from ASC: http://www.ausport.gov.au/__data/assets/pdf_file/0017/341072/Frontier_Research_The_Economic_Contribution_of_Sport_summary_report.pdf

Gandhi, M. K. (Mahatma). (1993, November 1). *Gandhi an autobiography: The story of my experiments with truth.* Boston, MA: Beacon Press.

Geisler, J. (2010). *What great bosses know about ethics traps.* Retrieved on July 12, 2010, from Poynter: http://www.poynter.org/how-tos/leadership-management/what-great-bosses-know/104258/what-great-bosses-know-about-ethics-traps/

Gentile, M. (2010). *Giving voice to values.* London, United Kingdom: Yale University Press.

Gilchrist, A. (2008). *True colours: My life*. Tuggerah, Australia: Pan Macmillan.

Gladwell, M. (2005). *Blink: The power of thinking without thinking.* New York, NY: Back Bay Books.

Grange, P. (2012). Bluestone Edge. www.bluestoneedge.com

Harrison, N. (2012). Psych Insight. www.psychinsight.com

Kidder, R. (2006). *Moral courage: Taking action when your values are put to the test.* New York, NY: HarperCollins.

Kotter, J. P., & Cohen, D. (2002). *The heart of change: Real life stories about how people change their organizations.* Boston, MA: Harvard Business Press.

Kotter, J. P., & Heskett, J. L. (1992). *Corporate culture and performance.* New York, NY: The Free Press.

Le Guin, U. K. (1973). In R. Silverberg (ed.), *The ones who walk away from Omelas* (Vol. 3), (A hard-cover science fiction anthology). United States: New Dimensions.

Longstaff, S. (2009). St James Ethics Centre, NSW, Executive Director.

Messick, D. M., & Tenbrunsel, A. E. (2004), Ethical fading: The role of self-deception in unethical behavior. *Social Justice Research 17*(2), 223–236.

Pinker, S. (1994, November 7). *Language instinct how the mind creates language* (1st ed.). New York, NY: William Morrow & Company.

Rest, J. R. (1986, November 7). *Moral development: Advances in research and theory.* Westport, CT: Praeger.

Rice, G. (1920's). *Alumnus football.*

Ross, W. D. (1930). *The right and the good.* Oxford, United Kingdom: Clarendon Press.

Samuels, A. (2001). *Politics on the couch.* New York, NY: Karnac Books.

Shockley-Zalabak. P. (1999). *Fundamentals of organizational communication: Knowledge, sensitivity, skills and values.* New York, NY: Addison-Wesley.

Singer, P. (1993). *Practical ethics* (2nd ed.). Cambridge, England: Cambridge University Press.

St. James Ethics Centre (n.d.). Retrieved from www.ethics.org.au

The Associated Press. (2012, October 23). CTV news *mired in Armstrong doping scandal, UCI claims moral authority to lead cycling.* Retrieved from http://www.ctvnews.ca/sports/mired-in-armstrong-doping-scandal-uci-claims-moral-authority-to-lead-cycling-1.1006812. Used with permission of The Associated Press Copyright © 2013. All rights reserved.

The Independent. (2013, May 23). Retrieved from http://www.independent.co.uk/sport/golf/as-the-sergio-garcia--tiger-woods-racismrow-escalates-we-ask-is-golf-racist-8628257.html Used with permission The Independent Copyright © (2013) www.independent.co.uk

Vincent Fairfax Fellowship (2010). (Ethics in Leadership) St James Ethics Centre.

Winnicott, D. (1953). Transitional objects and transitional phenomena. *International Journal of Psychoanalysis 34,* 89–90.

Index

CPSIA information can be obtained
at www.ICGtesting.com
Printed in the USA
LVHW051053010222
709871LV00015B/2338